TRADE-OFFS

TRADE-OFFS

An Introduction to Economic Reasoning and Social Issues

SECOND EDITION

HAROLD WINTER

THE UNIVERSITY OF CHICAGO PRESS

Chicago and London

HAROLD WINTER is professor of economics at Ohio University.

The University of Chicago Press, Chicago 60637
The University of Chicago Press, Ltd., London
© 2013 by The University of Chicago
All rights reserved. Published 2013.
Printed in the United States of America

22 21 20 19 18 17 16 15 14 13   1 2 3 4 5

ISBN-13: 978-0-226-92449-6 (paper)
ISBN-13: 978-0-226-92450-2 (e-book)
ISBN-10: 0-226-92449-1 (paper)
ISBN-10: 0-226-92450-5 (e-book)

Library of Congress Cataloging-in-Publication Data

Winter, Harold, 1960– author.
   Trade-offs : an introduction to economic reasoning and social issues /
Harold Winter.—Second edition.
      pages   cm
   Includes bibliographical references and index.
   ISBN-13: 978-0-226-92449-6 (paperback : alkaline paper)
   ISBN-13: 978-0-226-92450-2 (e-book)
   ISBN-10: 0-226-92449-1 (paperback : alkaline paper)
   ISBN-10: 0-226-92450-5 (e-book)   1. Economics.   2. Reasoning.
3. Economic policy.   4. Social policy.   5. Ethics.   I. Title.
   HB171.W764 2013
   330.01′156—dc23

                                                    2012022540

To Gwill Allen for getting me into economics,
Jeremy Greenwood for getting me into the
University of Rochester, and Eric Hanushek for
getting me out of the University of Rochester
(which was much more difficult than getting in).

Contents

Preface to the Second Edition

THE FIRST edition of *Trade-Offs* was published on the same day as another book about economic reasoning—*Freakanomics: A Rogue Economist Explores the Hidden Side of Everything*, by Steven Levitt and Stephen Dubner. While I thank the astute Amazon reviewer who titled his five-star review of my book "Infinitely Better than *Freakanomics*," *Trade-Offs* has not quite had the social (or sales) impact that other book has had. Don't get me wrong. I am not bitter that Levitt stole my thunder. Perhaps Levitt had a better title. Perhaps I too should have called myself a rogue economist, even though I have no clue what that means in terms of my writing, or Levitt's for that matter. Whatever the case, I was thrilled to see my book in print, especially for the University of Chicago Press.

Trade-Offs changed my life, and for the better. I had so much fun writing that book that I decided to write more books. To date, I have written and published two more books, one on the economics of crime and the other on the economics of addiction. With all of these books, I became extremely up to date on many economics topics I knew little or nothing about. As a result, I became a much better economist, and a much better teacher of economics. My main target audience has always been undergraduate students, especially my own, and I appreciate all the flattering comments I have received over the years from students and professors who have read my books.

When the University of Chicago Press asked me to write a second edition, I immediately agreed. With many economic texts, new editions come quite frequently, often every other year. The main reason for this is to make the previous edition obsolete in the marketplace, circumventing those pesky used book sales that cut into publisher profits. The University of Chicago Press does not share that philosophy, and neither do I. It has been seven years since the publication of the first edition, and the sole goal of writing a new edition is to add more interesting material that has become available during that time.

In deciding how to proceed with a new edition, I had to consider two important points. The first is that most of the readers of the new edition will not have read the previous one, so the fundamental introductory material covered in the first edition must remain as is. The second point is that a new edition has to be "new," so I decided to expand from within, updating many of the applications of economic reasoning I discussed in the first edition. I wanted to write the same book, but different, and still keep it at a length that works well as a supplemental text. If you have read the first edition, I hope you find the new material interesting and rewarding. If you haven't read the first edition, welcome to my world (and please read the preface to the first edition following this one).

So how is this edition different than the previous one? The first substantial change is that this edition is one chapter shorter. I decided to remove the products liability chapter to keep this edition from getting too big. Also, it was the only chapter that many readers said didn't fit well with the rest of the book—they thought the tone was too formal, and the material was more difficult. If you are a fan of the economics of products liability, however, don't worry. I have taken the key material from that chapter, condensed it, and added it to one of the chapters in this edition.

The next big change concerns the chapter on the individual decision to smoke. While the new chapter is still primarily about smoking, I have added some material on drinking and overeating. I have also tackled the topical and controversial issue of the "new paternalism," that is, social policy designed to protect people from themselves, but from an economic perspective. I knew very little about this topic when I wrote the first edition, but I was intrigued enough to eventually write a whole book on the topic of addiction and social policy. With the research I read to write that book, I have completely reworked and expanded the "smoking" chapter in this book.

There are two other major changes. The first involves a lengthy discussion of new research on the economics of infectious diseases, especially concerning the HIV/AIDS epidemic. Economists have some interesting and unusual things to say about policies designed to combat that epidemic. The second greatly expands the material on policies that deal with the shortage of organs available for transplants. I present new research on market and nonmarket solutions, including fascinating research on what is known as *kidney exchange*, a field of inquiry that has actually led to the saving of lives in the real world.

While these are the major changes, there are many more minor changes throughout the book. I have strived to add something new to almost every topic I cover, even if it is just a short expansion at times. As you will see from my chapter endnotes, there is plenty of new material that has been added that makes the second edition stand out from the first. At least that has been my sincere intention. Who knows, maybe I'll get to do this again in seven years. But even if not, I had as much fun writing this edition as I did the first. I hope you enjoy reading it.

Preface to the First Edition: Welcome to My World

HELLO. My name is Harold Winter and I am a professor of economics at Ohio University. My main field of interest is economics of law, and my job description involves basically two things—teaching and research. But as a bonus, I often get the opportunity to use economic reasoning to frighten people.

For example, a couple of years ago my mother was visiting me. I have a nice relationship with my mother, but we don't often talk about social issues. One night, however, she asked me what I had talked about in class that day. Usually I would have little to say about what I teach, especially when I am teaching formal economic theory courses. But that day was special: I was doing an independent reading course with a very bright student. We were reading a book about the American health care system written by an intense free-market-oriented legal scholar. In one of the chapters we discussed that day, the author argued that it may be sensible social policy to allow overworked emergency rooms to refuse care to patients who couldn't pay or who didn't have insurance. As I told my mother about this, I went into "professor mode" and ranted on for about ten minutes, showing her my passion for economic reasoning. When I was finished, she had a scared look in her eyes and then simply said, "You're a monster!"

Being called a monster by my mother didn't really bother me, but I started thinking about how completely alien economic reasoning is to some people. I think what surprises many people about economics is that it can be applied to an extremely broad range of issues. Most people expect economists to talk about unemployment, inflation, or the budget deficit, but not about organ transplants, cigarette addiction, or secondhand smoke. But economists can place just about any issue into an economic context, sometimes even to the surprise of other economists.

When I was a graduate student in Rochester, New York, I was once in a professor's office when his phone rang. From his end of the conversation, all I heard him say was: "I'll get there as soon as I can." After he hung up the phone he told me he had to leave immediately to be a consultant for a hospital in Boston. I jokingly asked him if they needed his permission to perform an operation. He said that was exactly what they needed. And he wasn't kidding! The doctors were deciding between some different procedures, and they wanted his opinion on the cost-effectiveness of each one. Can you imagine lying on an operating table and the surgeon tells you not to worry because the economist is on his way?

When using economic reasoning to approach social issues, the concepts of right and wrong can become very murky. I have always found this comforting. When I was young, whenever my parents told me I was wrong about something, I always responded by saying "from whose point of view?" Although that response rarely impressed my parents, I always maintained that the concepts of right and wrong were often a matter of perspective. As I became more exposed to economic reasoning, I came to realize that there is a whole academic discipline that shares this view. Instead of focusing on what is right or wrong, economists focus on costs and benefits.

Cost-benefit analysis allows economists to *detach* themselves not only from their personal views, but also from favoring one side or the other of whatever social issue is at hand. What this entails will be made clear as I discuss specific issues throughout this book, such as product safety, copyright protection, and secondhand smoke. I have my own personal opinions about some of these issues, but it is my professional opinion I intend to relate to you. The mantra I teach my students is this: *if you are on one side of an issue, you are on the wrong side.* I don't expect my students to accept this mantra in their personal lives, but I *require* them to accept it in my class.

In this book, I will be focusing primarily on theoretical issues as opposed to empirical issues or policy solutions. I am going to use many abstract and hypothetical situations to introduce you to economic reasoning. I am not going to present economic reasoning as a cure-all for real-world problems. My goal is far more modest. I simply want to present you with a unique way of thinking about social issues, one that allows you to sidestep some of the moral, ethical, or legal arguments that often are used in public policy debate. Keep in mind that in no way am I claiming that these other concerns are unimportant, and I recognize that they are generally at the forefront of public policy debate. I only want to present economic reasoning as *a* way of thinking about social issues, not *the* way of thinking about them. I do believe, however, that economic reasoning is an important and valid way of thinking about social issues.

Many of the topics I will discuss here have been analyzed in tremendous detail by many types of scholars. My goal is to introduce you to basic economic reasoning, and not to present you with a thorough discussion of all of these details. Furthermore, there are numerous issues I will not cover at all in an attempt to keep my presentation as concise as possible. If you are reading this book as a supplemental text in some policy course, I am sure you will appreciate my brevity. I will provide several references at the end of each chapter for the interested reader to further pursue the topics I discuss, and many others, in greater detail.

I wrote this book in conjunction with preparing a course in health economics, thus many of the issues I will discuss here are health related. Because the course was interdisciplinary in nature, my goal was to make the material accessible to students who had little or no background in economics. The material was presented with no graphs, no math, few statistics, and a few numerical examples when needed for ease of exposition. I will continue that approach throughout this book.

Throughout the years, I have had many discussions of social issues with friends, colleagues, students, and family members. I will relate some of these conversations to you, but usually keep the names of the other parties involved anonymous. In case my memory is faulty, I apologize to those other parties for possible misrepresentations of their views and comments. I assure you that my misrepresentation was done accidentally, unless it was done to be entertaining.

NOTE

The book on the American health care system is by Richard Epstein, *Mortal Peril: Our Inalienable Right to Health Care?* (Reading, MA: Addison-Wesley Publishing Co., 1997).

Acknowledgments

FOR THE SECOND EDITION, I want to thank David Pervin, senior editor at the University of Chicago Press, for making this second edition a reality. I also want to thank Kelly Finefrock-Creed for her excellent copyediting. Thanks also to Shenyun Wu, Melinda Kennedy, and everyone else at the press I have not met but who have helped with this edition.

A special thanks to Chris Matgouranis who was the most enthusiastic research assistant I have ever worked with.

I also want to thank my in-laws, Minda, Walter, and Francis, for helping out with Thomas, who easily could have prevented me from getting this book written. He faces no trade-offs in his life—he gets everything he wants. Enjoy it for now, boy, it will change soon.

Finally, and always, there is Jenn.

For the first edition, my first debt of gratitude goes to Alex Schwartz, senior editor at the University of Chicago Press. Throughout our correspondence, Alex's interest in this project and the encouragement he gave me was without bounds. I have never seen so much energy come from one person. I'm just glad he uses his powers for good instead of evil. I also got to work closely with Catherine Beebe and Mara Naselli. Catherine had the magic touch in picking reviewers, and Mara made my words sound like they were written by someone who knows how to write. Both demonstrated a phenomenal amount of enthusiasm for this project. I also appreciate their patience in dealing with the thousands of questions I asked along the way. And to Peter Cavagnaro and everyone else at the press who has contributed to the publication of this book, thanks for making this the most enjoyable publishing experience I have ever had.

As a student, I had the good fortune to have two academic mentors. Eric Hanushek, my graduate mentor and the nicest economist in the world, made important comments on an early version of this book that significantly affected the way I decided to write it. Gwill Allen, my undergraduate mentor who currently is an anticompetitive watchdog for the Canadian government, also provided helpful comments. These guys are economists' economists. Thanks for all your help over the years.

I have also had the good fortune to be the mentor of several excellent students. Three in particular, Jeff Baird, Ryan Richey, and Michael Taylor, have engaged me in many challenging discussions about economics and public policy. Thanks for keeping me sharp. I also want to thank the students who have taken my health economics course for their patience in watching me develop a new course. It was a great teaching experience for me. Thanks to Tiffany Margrave for assisting me in collecting readings for the course.

I also benefited from many conversations and comments from my colleagues at Ohio University. Early on in the writing process, I had many conversations about the material in this book over chicken wings with Donald Lacombe. Julia Paxton read the first draft of the book and let me know I was on the right track. Ariaster Chimeli, Charlene Kalenkoski, David Klingaman, and Rosemary Rossiter all read the manuscript and made helpful comments. Also, I thank Roy Boyd for giving me plenty of time to prepare the health economics course.

I owe a special debt of gratitude to William Neilson, my good friend and coauthor. Bill has taught me more about doing research than anyone else I know. His critical reading of the manuscript allowed me to make substantial improvements. And after all the reviews for this book were in, he asked me if his was the harshest. Yes it was, and I appreciate it.

I would also like to thank the anonymous reviewers for their thoughtful comments. Other reviewers who were not anonymous, Edward Foster, Joni Hersch, and Kate Wahl, are also greatly thanked.

I also want to thank my family for their never-ending support. My parents provided me with several stories for this book, my sister collected Canadian cigarette packages for me to use in show and tell in my classes, and my brother and his family listened to my rants on more than one occasion.

Finally, I want to thank Jenn for making me happy.

1   *Approaching Social Issues*

IN ANALYZING social issues, I was trained as an economist not to make moral judgments about right and wrong but to try to identify the trade-offs—that is, the costs and benefits—of whatever issue is at hand. I have seen many of my students struggle with this approach, not just in terms of performing well on their exams but in accepting it as a legitimate way to think about public policy. To introduce them to the economic way of thinking, I present an approach to resolving social issues that has three steps:

Step 1: Identify the theoretical trade-offs of the issue in question. This is the costs and benefits step, a concept that is very familiar to every economist. Regardless of the issue, there are always trade-offs to consider. Furthermore, for any policy solution proposed, there will be those in favor of it as well as those against it (and keep in mind, choosing one solution means foregoing another). If everyone could agree on the resolution of a social issue, it wouldn't be much of an issue in the first place. Economists have a way of identifying costs and benefits that few others would ever consider, largely due to our ability to detach ourselves from many of the personal concerns that can complicate policy analysis. We can argue in favor of drug abuse, obesity, theft, and even death. We can argue against safer products, pollution control, and drugs that improve the quality of life for individuals who have contracted HIV. In sum, economists are a lot of fun to talk to at parties.

Step 2: If possible, empirically measure the trade-offs to determine if the costs outweigh the benefits, or vice versa. If you are interested in proposing a policy solution, it helps to have some idea of the relative magnitude of the trade-offs you identified in step 1. To justify your solution, it generally will be useful to argue that the benefits of your solution outweigh the costs. How you want to measure the trade-offs is an important issue. You may just have a sincere gut feeling about the value of your solution, or you may want to pull out the serious statistical tools to support your claim. Either way, step 2 can be a difficult stage for several reasons.

First, empirical analysis requires data, which can come from several sources, such as surveys, observable market information, or controlled experiments. Unfortunately, data collection is often difficult to do, and as a result, data are often measured inaccurately. Second, the real world is a big and messy place to study. A lot of data that ideally would be needed to accurately measure trade-offs simply may not be available. Third, there are many different statistical methods that can be used to measure the same trade-offs. Advances in computer technology and statistical software have made it possible for almost anyone with a computer to do sophisticated empirical work, so you often get to see many different approaches to the same problem. Finally, not only can the empirical approaches differ in statistical techniques but also in empirical design. What data are most relevant? If there are alternative ways to measure the same variable, which measure should be used?

Fortunately, there are procedures that deal with many of these problems, and the best empirical work deals openly with these shortcomings. What I believe is most important for empirical work is to allow others to be able to verify the integrity of your data, and to be able to replicate your results. But this may not always be possible if there are proprietary rights that make the sharing of data impossible. Still, being able to examine the robustness of the results of any particular study is important in determining the value of that study. It is often the case that you can have a group of economists who are in complete agreement over step 1 but in complete disagreement over step 2. I should point out, however, that disagreement over step 2 in no way diminishes the value of economic reasoning. There are legitimate and passionate disagreements in how to measure trade-offs, but this simply is an unavoidable consequence of the nature of empirical work. Any academic discipline that attempts to apply empirical analysis to policy issues will have to confront these same problems.

Step 3: Recommend (or implement) social policy based on the first two steps. This may be the most exciting step if you are passionate about public policy. While there are some economists who are in the position to actually implement social policy, the bulk of public policy economic research is meant to imply, or recommend, policy solutions. Many economists keep their research largely to themselves and to a small group of scholars who are interested in the same issues. But some economists step out into the public arena and make their positions clear. The fun begins not only when other economists are right out there bumping heads with them, but when scholars and analysts from all walks of life are also thrown into the mix. Step 3 is where you get to flex your muscles and find out if anyone who is in a position to make policy decisions actually cares about what you have to say. This step is definitely the loudest of the three steps.

Taken together, I believe that these three steps present a reasonably coherent approach to public policy analysis: identify trade-offs, measure trade-offs, and recommend policy. These steps on their own, however, are still incomplete. They have no policy relevance until a policy *objective* can be identified.

OBJECTIVELY SPEAKING

As outlined above, many of the academic debates over public policy occur due to the difficulties associated with step 2, the empirical measurement of trade-offs. But there are also difficulties in pursuing the other two steps. It is one thing to say that we are going to identify trade-offs, but it is another thing to say exactly *which* trade-offs we are going to identify. In a perfect world, it would be nice to identify every conceivable cost and benefit associated with a policy solution, no matter how far-reaching the trade-offs may run. In practice, however, and even in theory, only the most relevant trade-offs are usually considered. And this, in turn, often depends on what policy objective is being considered.

If you are going to recommend or implement public policy, you need to have a policy objective. For example, let's assume that we *can* accurately and unambiguously identify and measure costs and benefits. This would appear to make policy analysis an easy task. Propose a policy solution. If the benefits of the solution outweigh the costs, adopt the solution. If not, abandon the solution. If there is more than one solution, find the one that has the greatest spread between benefits and costs. This is a common economic approach to public policy, as economists are often solely concerned with maximizing the spread between social benefits and social costs, or what is often referred to as *social welfare* (or social *wealth*) maximization.

If our policy goal is to maximize social welfare, we want to try to identify trade-offs that affect social welfare. For example, assume a new workplace safety regulation is being enforced in which a specific safety feature must be installed. A benefit of the regulation is that it may reduce worker injury or death. A cost of the regulation involves the resources that must be used to physically install and maintain the safety feature. Whatever trade-offs are identified, we can then move on to the next step and measure them.

In measuring trade-offs, it is common for economists to place a monetary value on all the relevant costs and benefits. For example, the installation of the safety feature will involve direct costs that are likely already measured in dollars. But there may be less direct costs, such as the value of lost production if the plant must be closed down while the feature is being installed, or if workers have to spend time in training sessions. Dollar equivalents can also be established for these costs. On the benefits side, a dollar value equivalent can be established for the value of lives saved or injuries avoided. Although this may seem coarse, all of the trade-offs we identify must be measured in the same units, such as dollars, to allow for a direct comparison of the costs and benefits of the safety feature. Thus, social welfare is often measured in dollars.

Even if there is agreement on the broad objective of maximizing social welfare, policy objectives may differ due to differences in the definition of social welfare. A good example of this can be found in the economic analysis of crime. To deter crime, we must use resources for the apprehension, conviction, and punishment of criminals. These costs are offset by the benefits in crime reduction. But should the benefits that accrue to individuals who commit crime (also members of society) be added to social welfare? If yes, this may suggest that fewer resources can be used to deter crime, because crime itself has offsetting benefits. If no, crime is more costly to society, and more resources may be needed for deterrence. Notice, however, that it is a *fact* that a criminal reaps a benefit from committing a crime (or why commit the crime?), yet it is an *opinion* as to whether that benefit should be counted as social welfare. Policy objectives and definitions of social welfare are *subjectively* determined. This accounts for why social issue debates are often extremely contentious.

What, then, should be counted as social welfare? Throughout this book, what counts as social welfare will depend on the specific topic of interest, whether it is safety regulation, copyright protection, secondhand smoke, and so on. Economists tend toward inclusiveness in defining social welfare. That is, they tend to be concerned about identifying the existence of costs and benefits, and not concerned about who reaps the benefits or incurs the costs. In other words, a dollar is a dollar, regardless of who gets the dollar. But this leads to another problem. Even if we can agree on all the trade-offs that should be included in social welfare, we may disagree on the appropriate social policy goal. For example, instead of only being concerned with welfare maximization (*efficiency*), we may also want to be concerned with how that wealth is distributed (*equity*).

Distribution of wealth issues can be very difficult to deal with. The concept of fairness tends to be open ended. For example, what if you and I are trying to split $1,000? If I suggest that we each get $500, I wouldn't be surprised if you considered that to be a fair split. But what if I am rich and you are poor? Maybe, then, to remedy that inequity you should get $750 and I get only $250. Wouldn't that be fair? But then again, if I am rich and you are poor, $250 may be as valuable to you as $750 would be to me. After all, we may want to consider how each dollar increases our levels of happiness *on the margin*. If a rich person is not likely to value one extra dollar as much as a poor person would, to be fair we may want the rich person to get more. The important point with this exercise is that one can rationalize *any* split of the $1,000.

In all, proposing policy solutions can lead to endless debate. Even if there is agreement on the objective of social welfare maximization, there may be disagreement as to what should be included in the definition of social welfare. And even if there is agreement over the definition, there may be disagreement over the appropriate goals of social policy. How, then, are we to proceed with the three-step approach to resolving social issues?

MY GAME PLAN

In this book, I am going to focus primarily on step 1. Identifying trade-offs is what I personally am most interested in doing as an economist, and I enjoy thinking abstractly about social issues. Furthermore, step 1 is the least contentious step among economists as there is generally a strong agreement over the identification of costs and benefits. Finally, step 1 is where economic policy analysis begins.

Although I will discuss many empirical studies throughout this book, the formal elements of step 2 will not be emphasized. I prefer to focus on the least contentious aspects of economic analysis. More to the point, the important debates over empirical work do not really involve the opposing results of the studies. Instead, the debates focus primarily on choice of data and statistical techniques. If you have some basic background in statistical economics, (what economists refer to as *econometrics*), discussing how empirical studies differ can be an important and fascinating exercise. I'm going to assume, however, that the typical reader of this book does not have such a background. If you do have further interest in empirical research, I will provide you with several references at the end of each chapter.

As for step 3, one thing I certainly will not do is to present my recommendations for policy solutions. What I personally think about public policy issues has absolutely no bearing on understanding basic economic reasoning. What I will do, however, is often consider the goal of social welfare maximization (that is, maximizing the spread between social benefits and social costs) as my policy objective. How social welfare is defined will depend on the specific issue at hand, and this will become clearer in the chapters to come. I will not, however, be concerned with distributive issues.

I do want to make it clear that in no way I am arguing that the objective of social welfare maximization is what policy decision makers actually *do* care about. The economics field of *public choice* addresses the issue of what policy makers do care about, and if you have further interest in that topic, I recommend that you find out more about that field. I am also not going to claim that social welfare maximization is the objective that policy makers *should* care about. There are many legitimate social policy goals, and what policy makers should care about is a matter of opinion.

My main reason for focusing on a specific economic objective is that it will allow me to place the trade-offs I identify into a policy context, and I believe that this will facilitate my presentation of economic reasoning. Try to think of identifying trade-offs in the context of social welfare maximization as an abstract exercise, designed to teach you how to think like an economist, not to teach you how to resolve complex, real-world social issues. Although the ultimate goal of policy analysis is to answer questions about how to resolve these issues, I want to focus on the first step toward that goal—*raising* the appropriate questions about trade-offs. No matter how you decide to measure trade-offs, or how you decide to consider trade-offs in any social policy objective context, *trade-offs always exist*. No amount of disagreement about public policy issues can ever change that fact.

NOTES

If you want to learn more about applying statistical techniques to economics, there is an excellent source by Peter Kennedy, *A Guide to Econometrics*, 6th ed. (Hoboken, NJ: Wiley-Blackwell, 2008).

For a thorough discussion of the use of efficiency and equity criteria in identifying social policy objectives, see the book by Louis Kaplow and Steven Shavell, *Fairness versus Welfare* (Cambridge, MA: Harvard University Press, 2002). Also, see the following book reviews: Daniel A. Farber, "What (If Anything) Can Economics Say about Equity?" *Michigan Law Review* 101 (2003): 1791–1823; David Dolinko, "The Perils of Welfare Economics," *Northwestern University Law Review* 97 (2002): 351–93; Ward Farnsworth, "The Taste for Fairness," *Columbia Law Review* 102 (2002): 1992–2026; and Jules L. Coleman, "The Grounds of Welfare," *Yale Law Journal* 112 (2003): 1511–37.

2   A Valuable Life (to Some Extent)

I ATTENDED A DINNER party several years ago that was also attended by a new professor in the Health Administration Department. Professors who are fresh out of graduate school are often wildly enthusiastic about intellectual discussions, and she was no exception. As we sat down to eat, all of a sudden she began to question me about economic studies that attempt to place a dollar value on human life. She had seen some of these studies in graduate school and was uncomfortable with the idea of equating a person's life with a finite dollar amount. She felt that a human life can only be infinitely valued, and she used the words *immoral* and *repulsive* to describe the studies that contradicted her view.

In response, I told her that I could easily convince her that she herself did not place an infinite value on her own life. She was confident that I couldn't convince her of any such thing, but she allowed me the opportunity to try. First, I asked her if she had driven to the dinner party that night. She said yes. I then asked her if she believed it was possible, even just slightly possible, for her to have been killed in an accident on her way to the party. Again, she said yes. Finally, I asked her why she would take even the slightest risk of losing her infinitely valued life, especially just to attend a dinner party. She thought about it for a minute and then conceded that I had a valid point. I hope she didn't think I meant that she should never leave her house again!

My point was that what some economists do explicitly, virtually every individual does implicitly—they place a finite value on human life. Economists, as well as other researchers, routinely use a *statistical value-of-life estimate* in policy analysis to measure trade-offs. This is the value of life in a cost-benefit analysis sense: the dollar cost of improved safety must be compared to the dollar benefit of improved safety. If the benefit is measured in lives saved, a dollar value of life is important to determine. This fact will be made painfully clear in the next section.

THE FORD PINTO

The Ford Pinto case represents a tragic example of the application of value-of-life estimates in a cost-benefit framework. On an Indiana highway in 1978, three girls between the ages of sixteen and eighteen were hit from behind while driving a Ford Pinto. The Pinto caught on fire, exploded, and killed two of the girls immediately; the other died a short time later from severe burns.

In an unprecedented move, the district attorney brought criminal charges of reckless homicide against Ford. Apparently, had Ford made an $11 modification in the design of the Pinto, the deaths of the girls may have been avoided. Furthermore, Ford was well aware of this, because its engineers had undertaken a cost-benefit analysis in which they had assigned a dollar value to the potential loss of human life in the event of just such an accident. The conclusion of the analysis was that it was more cost effective for Ford to pay damages to the families of accident victims than it was to make the modification. Thus, concluded the prosecuting attorney, Ford had arrogantly, and criminally, traded lives for dollars.

Exactly what did the Ford engineers do? To begin with, they calculated the cost of an $11 modification for the total number of Pintos on the road. This yielded an amount of approximately $138 million. Next, they determined how many individuals would probably be killed or injured in a rear-end Pinto collision, and using average liability amounts from wrongful death and injury litigation, they calculated their legal liability of not using the modification. Using a liability amount of $200,000 for each person killed, and another amount of $67,000 for each person injured, they totaled their overall liability at approximately $50 million. (This also included a small amount for the cost of the damaged Pintos.) Because the former figure dwarfed the latter one, Ford concluded that it would be cost effective *not* to use the modification but rather to pay civil liability when required to do so.

Even if you accept the cost-benefit analysis and the numbers Ford used, a common response about the Pinto case is: What was Ford thinking? Let's face it. Why not just put the $11 modification in the car and charge $11 more for a Pinto? Lives would be saved, and how could $11 more in the price of a Pinto really affect anyone? This is a very persuasive argument, but only if you do not delve deeper into the problem.

Have you ever considered how many thousands of decisions must go into something as complicated as product design for an automobile? There are so many margins for an automobile manufacturer to consider, many of which involve safety considerations. Any single improvement in safety may cost just a few dollars, but if there are hundreds of potential safety modifications to consider, the improvements in safety may cost thousands of dollars. And even if government regulations dictate minimum standards for a number of safety features, these decisions still have to be made by some agency. How, then, are these decisions to be made? What criteria should be used? If a safety feature involves lives saved, how are we to value those lives saved? As mentioned earlier, it is senseless to place an infinite value on human life. In that extreme case, the only real sound safety feature for an automobile would be not to produce any at all.

So what did Ford do wrong? Did it make a sound business decision? Quite possibly, yes. But a sound decision from Ford's perspective may not be a sound business decision from society's perspective. Proper cost-benefit analysis doesn't only require using a value-of-life estimate; it requires using the appropriate one. But what is meant by *appropriate*?

HOW VALUABLE IS A LIFE?

In a *wrongful death* case, part of the issue that must be determined by the judge or jury is how to assign a damage award for the loss of life. Although there are statutory differences across states, there are some common factors that are looked at to determine the damage award. Two broad categories of factors are damages based on *contributions* and damages based on *loss to the estate*. The first category primarily deals with the benefits that would have been provided for the decedent's beneficiaries had there been no wrongful death. The second category primarily deals with the probable earnings of the decedent, less probable personal expenses, had there been no wrongful death. Both of these factors focus on the *pecuniary* (or monetary) aspects of the loss, as opposed to the *nonpecuniary* aspects.

From a social perspective, a value of life includes anything that can be considered valuable to the individual. This tends to involve much broader categories than are included in a legal wrongful death damage determination. The goal of estimating a value of life, then, is to try to place a dollar value on both the pecuniary *and* nonpecuniary aspects of that value. How can this be done?

Individuals routinely take actions that suggest that they are willing to pay to *avoid*, or must be paid to *incur*, an increased risk of death. For example, if you buy a smoke detector for your home, you demonstrate that you are willing to pay a certain price to reduce the probability of being harmed or killed in a fire. Conversely, if you decide not to buy a smoke detector, you demonstrate that you are not willing to pay a certain price to be safer. In either case, your action can be used to infer a statistical value of your life.

To provide an example that is illustrative of a common approach economists use to estimate a value of life, let's consider an individual's decision process in choosing a job. Consider the following hypothetical situation. You are trying to choose between two job offers. Both jobs are completely identical to you except in two respects—one job has a slightly higher risk of death than the other job, and the wage rates may differ. Obviously, if you choose the riskier job it must be because you will be paid a wage premium relative to the less risky job. If you choose the less risky job, the wage premium will not be enough to compensate you for the increased risk. In this case, we may be able to identify the exact wage premium that makes you *completely indifferent* between the two jobs. With that amount, and some idea of the difference in the risk factors of the two jobs, we can estimate a value of life.

Let's make up some numbers to demonstrate the technique. Suppose the riskier job has a one in ten thousand (1/10,000) higher death risk than the less risky job. If I were to ask you, what is the minimum annual wage premium you would need to take that risk, how would you answer? If your answer is $500, this information tells me you need to be compensated $500 per 1/10,000 increase in the risk of dying. Now, if we think about 10,000 workers each giving an identical answer to the question, we have a total of ($500)(10,000), or $5 million, the workers are willing to pay to face, on average, one death from their group. (We say that there is *on average* one death in the group of 10,000 workers because there is a 1/10,000 chance of dying, but that does not mean there will be exactly one death.) In a statistical sense, then, we can say that one life is valued at $5 million. When I ask my students to perform a similar exercise, I get answers that range from $0 to $100 million. For the students who answer $0 and seemingly place no value on their lives, I try to discourage them from seeking careers as airline pilots.

Asking a hypothetical question about a risk choice that you would never explicitly consider in the real world may not be a very reliable way to determine a value-of-life estimate. Economists often use a more sophisticated method that involves using labor market data on the determinants of wage rates. A worker's wage depends on many factors, such as education, experience, type of industry, union status, fatality and injury risks, and several other things. Fortunately, there is a tremendous amount of data that exists on all of these variables for thousands of workers. A statistical technique allows the researcher, in effect, to compare workers with *identical* characteristics across every dimension except job fatality risk, and then determine the wage differential for a corresponding risk differential. If it is found, for example, that a $500 annual wage premium is needed to compensate for a 1/10,000 risk premium, the statistical value-of-life estimate for an average worker is calculated (just as above) to be $5 million.

The main advantage of using labor market data to estimate a statistical value of life is that we are using data based on observable market behavior. We are not asking a hypothetical question. Instead, we are observing wage/risk trade-offs that workers make in determining their optimal employment decisions. We must be careful, however, to take note that it is possible that workers, in general, do not have a good idea about the magnitude of the risks they face. If a worker underestimates the true risk of death, the amount needed to be compensated for accepting that risk *undervalues* the true statistical value of life. Furthermore, workers are not identical. Two workers facing the same risk may require different amounts of compensation. Thus, a statistical value of life found using data from one specific group of workers may not be an accurate value for another group of workers.

There have been numerous empirical studies that have attempted to estimate a statistical value of life. Many of these studies have proceeded along the same lines but have used numerous different data sets. While it is impossible for all of these various studies to reach exactly the same value-of-life estimate, the range of estimates is generally between $3 million and $9 million. Furthermore, there is a general belief that the typical wrongful death damage estimate usually (grossly) underestimates the statistical value-of-life estimate found in most empirical studies.

Returning to the Pinto case, the problem with Ford's cost-benefit analysis was not that it was trading lives for dollars. That necessarily must be done in designing products that may be used in ways that create the possibility of injuries or death. From its perspective, Ford correctly determined what it expected its legal liability to be largely based on the $200,000 wrongful death damage estimate that the courts used. However, if the social value-of-life estimate falls even in the lower end of the $3 million to $9 million range, the dollar cost of not adding the safety modification in terms of life lost and injury would be close to $1 billion. This outstrips the $50 million cost estimate used by Ford by a factor of twenty! With the larger value-of-life estimate, the conclusion of the cost-benefit analysis shows that the additional safety modification would have been cost effective and should have been implemented. Thus, Ford would have had to face a higher amount of liability to provide it with the incentive to add the safety feature. But this was more of an issue for product liability law or automobile safety regulation than it was for criminal law. Ford was ultimately acquitted of all criminal charges.

SCARCITY

If you accept the notion that there is a finite value of life for cost-benefit purposes, you necessarily accept the notion of trading lives for dollars. This implies that there are some safety features that simply are not cost effective. But what value-of-life estimate should you use? If too low a value is placed on the value of life, many safety features would be deemed not cost effective. If too high a value is used, too many safety features would be considered cost effective. But can you ever really have *too many* safety features? If we are not confident in the value-of-life estimate, shouldn't we at least use a high value so that we bias our results in favor of increased safety? The high end of the labor market estimates is $9 million. Is that the best estimate to use? Why not $12 million, or even $20 million? Let's be extremely safe and go as high as $50 million. In that case, any safety measure that costs less than $50 million per life saved should be implemented. Is this economically sound?

Suppose you are in a position to allocate state health insurance payments, and you have to make a choice between spending $5 million to keep a comatose child alive for at most one month or using the $5 million to give ten sick children life-saving operations. Which would you choose? My mother once gave me a very compassionate answer to this question: "I'd keep the comatose child alive *and* give the ten children their operations." That's a very nice answer, but it can lead to a follow-up question: What if the $5 million used to keep the child alive for one month can be used to save another ten children? If you answer that you should spend all $15 million, I can ask the same follow-up question again, and again. There will always be trade-offs to consider.

In the very first economics course I took, on the first day of class the professor defined economics to be the study of the allocation of *scarce* resources. If resources were not scarce, we could have practically everything we wanted—there would be few trade-offs to consider. A convenient way to think about resources is to use a monetary equivalent. A value-of-life estimate is a monetary value, but it corresponds to something concrete—a life. When I talk about spending $5 million to save ten children, the $5 million really refers to the value of the resources used in the life-saving operations. These resources are scarce, and there are only so many resources we as a society can spend on safety, or education, or defense, and so on. Every dollar of resource we spend somewhere is one dollar less we can spend elsewhere. This is why it is important to carefully consider where the dollars are spent, even when considering saving lives.

A value-of-life estimate is a useful benchmark to use in making safety decisions. For example, a 1985 Federal Aviation Administration regulation that implemented an aircraft cabin fire protection standard cost $100,000 per life saved. In this case, pretty much any statistical value-of-life estimate you use would suggest that the regulation is extremely cost effective. At the other extreme, a 1978 Occupational Safety and Health Administration (OSHA) regulation that implemented an arsenic occupational exposure limit cost $127 million per life saved. Even if you use the very high end of the value-of-life estimates, the cost of this regulation does not appear to be justified. But what if you simply refuse to accept the concept of a *cost-justified* safety feature? You wouldn't be alone: the US Supreme Court would be standing right behind you!

In a landmark 1981 case involving cotton dust standards, the Supreme Court ruled on the interpretation of the Occupational Safety and Health Act with respect to cost-benefit analysis:

The Act directs the Secretary to issue the standard that "most adequately assures . . . that no employee will suffer material impairment
of health," limited only by the extent to which this is "capable of being
done." In effect then . . . Congress itself defined the basic relationship
between costs and benefits, by placing the "benefit" of worker health
above all other considerations save those making attainment of the
"benefit" unachievable. . . . Thus cost-benefit analysis by OSHA is
not required by the statute because feasibility analysis is.

The implication of this ruling is that if a safety feature that reduces
the risk of injury to a worker is technically feasible, the cost of that
safety feature is not relevant in terms of policy implementation. If
you take this ruling literally, why not simply abolish the American
cotton industry? This is technically feasible, and it would reduce the
risk of cotton dust–related illness to zero. If you believe that abolish-
ing a whole industry for the sake of worker safety is unwarranted,
once again you accept the notion that there is a trade-off between
lives and dollars. The manner in which you could resolve this trade-
off, however, remains the interesting question.

It is unlikely that OSHA completely ignores costs in determining
occupational safety standards. The most likely effect of the Supreme
Court's ruling is that much more weight will be placed on the benefit
of occupational safety features compared to the costs of such features.
This may account for why regulations that cost over $100 million per
life saved are routinely proposed and sometimes enacted.

On the other hand, sometimes a government agency can catch
you off guard and do something completely unexpected with a
value-of-life estimate—it can lower it. In May 2008, the Environmental Protection Agency (EPA) was using a value-of-life estimate
of $6.9 million in assessing its regulatory policies. This value was
down $900,000 from a value of $7.8 million the EPA used in previous years. When the Associated Press discovered this change, a slight
controversy arose.

It may not be well understood by the public at large that government agencies even use a value-of-life estimate, and there is often a negative reaction to that fact. But even if understood, the EPA actually lowering the value may be thought of as a repugnant act. One serious criticism over the change is that it showed the Bush administration's willingness to devalue the role of environmental regulation. With a lower value-of-life estimate, as we saw in the Ford Pinto case, the benefits of additional safety features or regulation are also lower. The EPA, however, defended its position by arguing that it was simply updating the estimate based on the most recent value-of-life studies it could find. Whatever the case, the best studies have always offered a range of estimates, and whether or not it made good economic sense to lower the value, the EPA's actions provide an excellent illustration of how value-of-life estimates have real-world practical, and controversial, uses.

SOME ADDITIONAL THOUGHTS

To end this chapter, I would like to return to the Ford Pinto case to reflect on a few additional points. That case provides an excellent example of the difference between *private* costs and *social* costs. Ford was concerned with the private cost of its decision not to include the additional safety feature, and this cost largely hinged on how the courts assessed the value of life. But if the courts' assessment was well below the true social value of life, Ford's best private decision could diverge from the best social decision. Much of the law is concerned with this problem. If nobody in the world ever bothered anyone else, there would be little need for laws. But individual decisions are often made without explicit acknowledgement, or with poor information, of how one's decision may impact another. One role of social policy, then, is to try to provide incentives for private parties to take into account the social costs they may impose on others. This will be a common theme throughout the book.

The Pinto case also provides an example of how to evaluate a tragedy from a social perspective. The Pinto accident was a horrible tragedy. Three girls were killed and their families and friends were devastated. But a tough question remains: Does the Pinto accident create a motivation for additional social control of automobile safety standards? In this case, the answer may be yes. Ford decided against the additional safety feature, because it took into consideration the court-determined liability damages, which may have been a gross underestimate of the true social value of life. In this sense, the accident may have alerted us to reevaluate the social costs and benefits of Ford's decision.

In general, however, many tragic accidents do not rise to the level of a social tragedy. If a train derails and many people are killed, this accident does not necessarily tell us that railway safety standards were inadequate. Regardless of the comprehensiveness of safety standards, there is always a chance that a train may derail. The goal of eliminating all risks of injury or death is a noble one but simply not realistic. The main reason for this is that the cost of additional risk reductions will, before too long, become prohibitive. But even if you don't consider the costs of additional safety features, in most situations it will be technically infeasible to lower the accident rate to zero, short of banning all potentially risky activities.

Trying to determine if a tragic accident rises to the level of a social tragedy demonstrates another aspect of economic reasoning. It is not that economists ignore the substantial costs of a tragedy like the Pinto accident or a train derailment. Quite the contrary. Our goal is to try to measure the costs as accurately as possible, without being biased or overwhelmed by the nature of the tragedy in and of itself. Regardless of the nature of the tragedy, the ultimate question that must be answered in designing social policy for health and safety issues is this: What is the *optimal* accident rate in any given risky situation? The answer to this question must ultimately involve some form of cost-benefit analysis that trades lives for dollars, regardless of how much importance you place on the costs or benefits being considered.

Finally, we have talked about the Pinto case in terms of a technological safety feature. If Ford lacked the proper social incentive to install the feature, we can argue that there is a role for social policy to impose that incentive either through regulation or civil liability through the tort system. But safety is not just a technological problem. Consider more detailed facts of the Pinto case. Before they were hit from behind, the girls were stopped on a highway with no shoulder to retrieve a gas cap they had forgotten to replace after filling up with gas. Are they at least partially to blame for the accident? What about the driver of the van who supposedly was distracted and not watching the road? Was he partially to blame? Technology can only help so much: human behavior is also a big factor in determining the accident rate. Furthermore, improved technological features may adversely affect human behavior, possibly leading to the strange result that additional safety features may actually *increase* the accident rate. I will discuss these issues in later chapters.

NOTES

A leading economic researcher on value-of-life estimates and the economics of safety is W. Kip Viscusi. There are several excellent sources of his that have contributed to this chapter (and to several other chapters). For an extensive survey, see the article "The Value of Risks to Life and Health," *Journal of Economic Literature* 31 (1993): 1912–46. For a textbook treatment, see W. Kip Viscusi, John M. Vernon, and Joseph E. Harrington, *Economics of Regulation and Antitrust*, 4th ed. (Cambridge, MA: MIT Press, 2005).

Viscusi has also written about the Ford Pinto case in *Reforming Products Liability* (Cambridge, MA: Harvard University Press, 1991). For an interesting general book on the case, see Lee Patrick Strobel, *Reckless Homicide? Ford's Pinto Trial* (South Bend, IN: And Books, 1980).

For a legal description of factors considered in calculating wrongful death damages, see Restatement (Second) of Torts § 925: Actions for Causing Death.

The citation for the Supreme Court case on cotton dust standards is American Textile Manufacturers Institute, Inc. v. Raymond J. Donovan, Secretary of Labor, United States Department of Labor, 452 U.S. 490 (1981).

3 Do You Want to Trade?

WHILE I WAS LIVING in College Station, Texas, many years ago, the local newspaper had an interesting article on how smart grade school children can be. A reporter wanted to investigate whether young children were eating healthy food. The reporter interviewed children who had in their lunch boxes healthy snacks, such as fruit, instead of junk food snacks, and asked, "Do you ever trade your healthy snacks for junk food?" If I remember the story correctly, the children unanimously said, "No." The conclusion the reporter drew was that these children preferred to eat healthy snacks.

I hate to debunk a story about smart children, but there is probably a much simpler explanation for the reason why the children with the healthy snacks were not trading with the children with the junk food snacks. Put yourself in the position of a ten-year-old with a Snickers bar. Another child approaches you holding a banana and asks you to trade your Snickers bar for the banana. What would you do? My guess is that you would not find it to your advantage to give up your Snickers bar for a banana. It has nothing to do with the other child wanting to eat healthy food. Instead, it has everything to do with you not wanting to trade a candy bar for some fruit.

For trade to occur, *both* parties must find the transaction to be mutually advantageous. Economists refer to this as *gains from trade*. Let's say I have a used car to sell, and I would sell it as long as I can get at least $3,000. If I'm offered anything less than $3,000, I would rather keep the car. Assume that there are two potential buyers for my car. I may have no idea how much each buyer is willing to offer me for my car, but each of them must have some maximum amount that they are willing to pay. Let's say the first buyer is willing to pay at most $2,500, and the second buyer is willing to pay at most $3,500. With these amounts, the first buyer and I could negotiate for days, but we would never come to an agreement. The most buyer 1 is willing to pay falls $500 short of the lowest amount I am willing to accept. Buyer 1 and I have no gains from trade.

With buyer 2 it is a different story. We don't know each other's values, but through negotiation we are very likely to come to an agreement on some price between $3,000 and $3,500. Gains from trade exist between buyer 2 and me, and the dollar amount of those gains is $3,500 − $3,000, or $500. This means that at whatever price we agree upon, we will share the $500. The closer the price is to $3,500, the greater the share of the gains I receive. The closer the price is to $3,000, the greater the share of the gains buyer 2 receives.

One of the key implications of gains from trade is that they allow the resource to be transferred to a *higher-valued use*. If, like many economists, you are concerned with economic efficiency, the objective of moving a resource to a higher-valued use is one that you can embrace. But it must be noted that value is a subjective concept. I value my used car at $3,000. Buyer 1 values it at $2,500, and buyer 2 values it at $3,500. There is no right or wrong to these values. They are simply how much each individual, for whatever reasons, subjectively values the car.

The concept of subjective value is central to economic reasoning, yet to the noneconomist it is sometimes poorly appreciated. I believe this is because people often have the tendency to implicitly impose their own subjective values on others. For example, have you ever seen a friend buy something you thought was ridiculously expensive? Did you think to yourself that your friend was being ripped off or maybe just being foolish? But if your friend was willing to pay the price for the product, there necessarily must have been gains from trade from that purchase. Your friend and the seller must have both benefited from the transaction, or else it wouldn't have occurred. You may not have experienced gains from trade from the same transaction, but you weren't the one making the purchase.

I also believe the confusion about the term *value* comes from its common use as a synonym with the word *price*. How many television commercials have you seen that refer to a low price as a great value? But the term *value*, as I'm using it, has very little to do with the price of a product. While the price establishes a minimum value a buyer must have to be willing to purchase the product, the price itself tells us nothing about the maximum amount that buyer would be willing to pay. And it is this maximum amount that establishes a buyer's value for the product.

The concept of mutually advantageous gains from trade provides the main justification for supporting the existence of markets. For example, the used-car market allows me to sell my car to someone who values it more than I do. I don't need to know how much a potential buyer values my car, and the buyer doesn't need to know how much I value my car. The market simply allows us both to take advantage of our gains from trade. This is exactly what the well-known concept of the *invisible hand* refers to. Furthermore, as long as I am free to sell my car to whomever I want, I will never sell to someone who values it less than I do. Thus, a market encourages the movement of a resource to a higher-valued use, but prevents the movement of a resource to a lower-valued use.

Unfortunately, the invisible hand is sometimes missing a finger or two. For example, if buyer 2 doesn't know I have a car for sale, we will never get together to exploit those gains from trade. Also, even if buyer 2 knows about my car, it may be too costly for us to physically negotiate a deal. Travel costs, time costs, schedule conflicts, and so on, are all part of a broad category economists refer to as *transactions costs*. If the transactions costs are high, gains from trade may not be exploited. Information costs and transactions costs are often referred to as *market failures*, and are sometimes put forth as justifications for nonmarket alternatives to allocating resources. In some situations, even if no market failure is identified, the concept of a market existing in and of itself is thought of as inappropriate, or even worse.

CELLS FOR SALE

In the 1980s, an important property rights case slowly worked its way through the California court system. *Moore v. The Regents of the University of California* had all the drama of a made-for-television movie. Here are the facts of the case. In 1976, Moore was diagnosed with hairy cell leukemia, a very rare form of cancer. He was referred to Dr. Golde, practicing at the Medical Center of the University of California, Los Angeles (UCLA). Golde recommended that Moore's enlarged spleen be removed, and Moore agreed and signed a consent form. Prior to the surgery, Golde arranged to use portions of Moore's spleen to conduct research. That turned out to be an incredibly lucrative foresight on Golde's part.

The operation was successful, for both Moore and Golde. As Moore continued to recover, Golde continued to conduct research with Moore's cells. Furthermore, Golde insisted on Moore continuing to travel from his home in Seattle to UCLA to withdraw samples of blood, skin, bone marrow, and other material. As Moore became reluctant to continue making the trip, Golde offered to cover his expenses. Golde's generosity, however, was not purely in the best interest of his patient. With Moore's cells, Golde's research eventually led to the commercial development of a cell line and products derived from it that had a market value estimated to be approximately $3 billion. Moore eventually became suspicious of Golde's behavior, and especially of his insistence on having Moore sign more consent forms. Moore hired a lawyer, discovered the phenomenal market value of products derived from his cells, and filed a law suit against Golde and UCLA.

The main issue the court faced was to determine who would be given the property right to the cells—Moore or Golde. Because the cells had already been developed into a commercial product line, the impact of the court's decision on the litigants would primarily be one of equity, not efficiency. Would Moore be given the retroactive property right to extremely valuable cells? But for similar future cases, the court's decision could affect the allocation of resources, that is, would the cells end up being used for medical research? So to analyze this case, let's put it into a slightly different perspective.

Let's say you have a diseased spleen and need to have it removed to save your life. Your doctor informs you that it is possible that your spleen may yield some material that can be used to develop pharmaceutical products worth a tremendous amount of money. If you are given the property right over the spleen, the doctor cannot use the spleen without your consent. If the doctor is given the property right over the spleen, you have no say in how it is used once it is removed. Of course, you have the right to refuse medical treatment (an issue the court dealt with in the Moore case). But let's assume you prefer not to die, so with or without the property right, you have your spleen removed. Now, before any medical treatment is given, the court must assign the property right. What should it do?

In the Moore case, the first appeals court assigned the property right to Moore and offered the following explanation:

> We are told that if plaintiff is permitted to have decision making authority and a financial interest in the cell-line, he would then have the unlimited power to inhibit medical research that could potentially benefit humanity. He could conceivably go from institution to institution seeking the highest bid, and if dissatisfied, would claim the right simply to prohibit the research entirely. We conclude that, if informed, a patient might refuse to participate in a research program. We would give the patient that right. As to defendant's concern that a patient might seek the greatest economic gain for his participation, this argument is unpersuasive because it fails to explain why defendants, who patented plaintiff's cell-line and are benefiting financially from it, are any more to be trusted with these momentous decisions than the person whose cells are being used. . . . If this science has become science for profit, then we fail to see any justification for excluding the patient from participation in the profits.

Moore was a very rich man, at least for a few minutes. The California Supreme Court decision, however, reversed the previous court's ruling in large part due to the fear that giving the patient property right over important research materials would make it more costly to obtain the materials and thus hinder such research. Moore was no longer very rich, but at least he did have his health.

Although there are many issues raised by this case—legal, ethical, moral, and so on—the main economic issue involves seeing that the cells end up in their highest-valued use. Both appeals courts also seemed concerned with this issue, as each considered how their decision would affect medical research. In this particular case, however, it doesn't matter how either court ruled. Both decisions are correct.

What happens if the court awards the property right to the doctor? The doctor removes the spleen and keeps it for research purposes. The cells can be used to develop as many pharmaceutical products as possible. The patient gets no financial compensation. End of story. What happens if the court awards the property right to the patient? The doctor removes the spleen and keeps it for research purposes. The cells can be used to develop as many pharmaceutical products as possible. The patient becomes filthy rich. End of story.

But haven't we missed something? If the patient is given the property right over the cells, how does the doctor end up with them? Ask yourself this simple question: How long would it take me to sell my already-removed diseased spleen to the doctor, possibly for millions of dollars? Your answer to that question explains how the doctor ends up with the spleen.

The real issue in this case is not where the spleen ends up. The gains from trade are just too enormous for the doctor not to end up with the spleen. We are talking about a market value in the *billions* of dollars. Unless the patient with the property right has a serious problem with allowing his removed spleen to be used for medical research (and make no mistake, it must be a *very* serious problem), the lure of huge financial gains will have him gladly sell his spleen. The real issue seems to be one of equity. Should the doctor have to pay for the spleen? If the only objective is to move the resource to its highest-valued use, it doesn't matter if the doctor has to pay or not. The same financial lure that has the patient gladly selling his spleen has the doctor gladly buying it. But it may matter to others, and it will certainly matter to the doctor and the patient.

There is something about body parts, profits, and medical ethics that does not mix well for some people. Maybe there are important noneconomic considerations that affect how you feel about who should be given the property right over the cells. But the economic point is that, in spite of these other considerations, it doesn't matter who gets the property right—the cells end up being used for medical research. So using whatever criteria you prefer to assign the property right, you can rest assured that the final resting place of the cells is with the doctor.

As abhorrent as some people find it to discuss property rights and the selling of body parts, it's hard to imagine anyone disagreeing that a diseased spleen, once removed, should not be used for medical research. But what if a healthy spleen can be used for medical research? Would you be willing to sell your healthy spleen if you had the property right to do so? For me, if a doctor offered me millions of dollars for my spleen, I'd quickly say yes and throw in one of my kidneys as a bonus.

On a more serious note, the kidney issue is important, as there is a severe shortage of kidneys available for transplant to patients who may die without the operation, yet it is illegal to sell one of your kidneys, even though you can lead a healthy life with just one remaining kidney. It is also illegal to sell potentially life-saving organs from the recently deceased. Could allowing a market for the selling of organs help alleviate the severe shortage? Economists often champion such free-market ideas, despite the moral outrage such market solutions often elicit. Yet economic reasoning can also be used to support non-market solutions to the organ transplant problem, perhaps eliciting even greater moral outrage. The organ shortage issue will be addressed throughout the rest of this chapter.

HOW MUCH FOR YOUR KIDNEY?

On its website, the National Kidney Foundation reports that in the United States in 2008 the total number of transplants for kidneys, pancreases, livers, hearts, lungs, and intestines was 27,965. Yet as of November 2009, the waiting list for all of these organs totaled 107,046. Specifically for kidneys, by far the most common of organ transplants, there were 16,250 transplants in 2008, and 82,364 on the waiting list in 2009. If there is one fact that is widely known among public policy scholars in a number of fields, and among health care professionals and officials, it is that there is a severe shortage of organs available for transplant in the United States and many people die while on a waiting list. The current system of supplying organs for transplant by donation only has clearly failed, and there have been numerous suggestions put forth on how to alleviate this shortage.

While the various policy options all have a common goal of increasing the supply of organs, the options differ in other goals involving moral, ethical, and legal arguments. When you think about an "economic" solution, however, the first place an economist may think to look is toward establishing a market for the selling of organs. Although it is possible, in theory, to establish a market for the selling of cadaveric organs, this would have some obvious complications.

You could be paid today to deliver your organs in the future, but the condition of your organs and the circumstances of your death become uncertainties that may be difficult to price. Will your organs be in healthy condition? Will you die in a hospital so your organs can be immediately harvested, or will you die in a remote place not allowing the retrieval of your organs to be done in a timely manner? Or perhaps a payment can be made to your estate once your cadaveric organs have been successfully harvested and transplanted. This, however, may not give you a strong enough incentive to sell your organs. Another option would be to allow your surviving family members to transact a market exchange, although being concerned with selling organs immediately at the time of death of a loved one may be more than most people are willing to consider.

Whether these complications can be overcome, there is one potential market setting that is far more promising to consider—the market for kidneys. As already mentioned, you can live a healthy life with just one kidney, so if you are willing to part with a kidney, you can personally participate in the market transaction. This represents a classic gains from trade setting. Although there are several important issues to consider when developing a market for kidneys, I want to consider (arguably) the most important one—what would be the market clearing price for a kidney? One economic study directly addresses this issue.

To calculate the price of a kidney, the authors of the study estimate the minimum price an individual would be willing to accept to sell a kidney, assuming that there would be many potential sellers and that no individual seller would be able to set a price much higher than anyone else. They consider that the postsurgery cost of giving up a kidney has three main components: the risk of dying, the lost time during the recovery period, and the reduced quality of life. The goal now is to place a monetary equivalence value on each of these components.

First, they determine that the risk of dying during a kidney transplant is approximately 1/1,000. Using a dollar value (2005 dollars) of $5 million for their value-of-life estimate, they calculate that the average (or expected) loss of life equals (1/1,000) multiplied by $5 million, or $5,000. Second, they calculate the cost to an average person of a four-week postsurgery recovery period in terms of foregone earnings to be $2,700. Finally, although difficult to do, they attempt to place a monetary value on the reduced quality of life one may experience after have one kidney removed. For some, this may be quite low as you can typically lead a normal life with one kidney. But to the extent that you are physically active, and there is evidence that kidney donors may experience high blood pressure, there is likely to be some quality of life reduction. The authors assume this value to be $7,500. Putting all three values together, they estimate a total monetary cost to donors who give up a kidney to be $15,200, suggesting that this would be close to the market clearing price if a market for selling kidneys were to be established.

Although there are many criticisms toward establishing a market for kidneys that have been raised, I'd like to address just two of them, both relating to the impact of such a market on lower-income individuals. The first criticism is that the additional cost of the kidney would be a substantial financial burden on this group of people, making it more difficult for them to acquire a kidney. Certainly, an additional $15,200 can be constraining, but let's put things into the proper perspective. The estimated cost of a kidney transplant operation (in 2005 dollars) is $160,000, not including the price of the kidney. If individuals do not have adequate insurance coverage, or if they cannot afford the $160,000, adding another $15,200 on top is irrelevant. For those individuals who can afford the cost of the operation and the kidney, the additional price for the kidney is also irrelevant in terms of the transplant being performed.

This leaves us with one last group, those who can afford the cost of the surgery but not the additional cost of the kidney. This gap between $160,000 and $175,200 is unlikely to affect many people, but even if it does, consider the alternative of not being able to get a kidney due to a supply shortage. The price of a kidney in this case is, in effect, infinite. Even if there are individuals who are priced out of the kidney transplant market due to the additional $15,200, how many more individuals will get kidneys due to the expected large increase in supply?

While the first criticism focuses on the demand side of the kidney market, the second criticism focuses on the supply side. By allowing kidneys to be sold, the argument is that it is the lower-income people who would be most seduced into selling their kidneys. Thus, there would be a discriminatory factor on the supply side of the market that does not favor the poor. From an economic standpoint, it is difficult to place much concern on this criticism. Even if true, don't the poor people experience gains from trade when selling a kidney? In other words, *both* buyers and sellers of kidneys benefit from the market exchange. In this sense, lower-income people, or anyone for that matter, actually prefer to be able to sell their kidneys.

Perhaps the criticism is trying to be more subtle by suggesting that poor people may tend to make rash decisions for the immediate gain, eventually regretting they have sold a kidney. This can be a problem with *any* product, but there is a context in which it may be more of an issue of concern. Although you can live a healthy life with just one kidney, depending on your lifestyle, you may have to take more care in certain aspects of your daily routine. You may decide to sell a kidney today with the intention of living a healthier lifestyle in the future, only to find out that you do not follow through with your plans. This is similar to a person who starts to smoke cigarettes with the intention of quitting in a few years, but when the few years pass, that person decides not to quit. This type of behavior can lend itself to social policy control to protect people from themselves, and this will be discussed in greater detail in chapter 5.

IT'S NOT MY DEFAULT

While establishing a market for the selling of kidneys sounds like the quintessential economic idea, it is not the only approach economists have examined for alleviating the shortage of organs for transplant. It is also not the only approach that has faced severe scrutiny. In 2009, law school professor Cass Sunstein, at that time President Obama's nominee to head the Office of Information and Regulatory Affairs (OIRA), stepped into the public eye with his proposal for alleviating the organ shortage problem. His idea was to adopt a policy known as *presumed consent*, which presumes everyone to be organ donors unless they explicitly opt out of the program. This is the opposite of the system we currently have in place, which presumes everyone not to be donors unless they explicitly opt into the program.

Presumed consent is not a new idea, and it has been adopted in several countries such as Spain, Austria, and Sweden. Sunstein's proposal was met with mixed concerns by the press, but there were some harsh comments that gave the impression that the Obama administration would be sending agents out at night to snatch organs from people who did not realize their organs were presumed to belong to the state. Although that would make a fascinating movie, what Sunstein was proposing was simply to change the *default* from not being a donor to being a donor but still allow people to make their own choices.

Defaults provide an interesting setting in which to study how social policy can be designed to take advantage of what is considered to be a quirk in human behavior—the tendency of some people to stay put regardless of what "staying put" entails. Let's say you want to be an organ donor. Under the current system of donation only, the default is that you are not a donor, so you choose to opt into the program. If the default is changed under presumed consent, then you choose not to opt out of the program. To you, the default does not affect your ultimate decision—you remain an organ donor. If everyone was like you, changing the default would have no impact on the number of organ donors.

But not everyone is like you, and policy officials know this. Some people who choose not to opt into the organ donor program under the current default would also choose not to opt out of the program if the default was changed to presumed consent. It's not being an organ donor that matters to them; it's not wanting to opt out of the default, *regardless* of the default, that matters. This phenomenon is known as the *status quo bias*. Why do some people always choose to stay with the status quo?

The first explanation may simply involve the costs of switching being too high. If you have to do something specific to switch, such as fill in paperwork or go to some place to apply, you may find it best to stick with the default and save on those costs. While this is an obvious explanation, what is interesting about status quo bias is that there is evidence that it occurs even when switching costs are quite low.

Related to this explanation, it may not be the physical costs of switching that matter but the information costs. Perhaps you don't realize there is another option or what the default is to begin with. In countries that use presumed consent, do the people realize they are organ donors with the option of opting out of the program? In many cases, however, like the switching costs, the information costs are very low, yet the status quo bias exists. For example, even when people know they must choose a medical insurance plan at work, and they are aware of all the options, changing the default can have an impact on the frequency of plans chosen.

A third explanation involves what is referred to as the *omission/ commission bias*. In this case, people may care more about making errors of commission (regretting an option that was chosen instead of the default) than they do about making errors of omission (regretting an option that was the default). The idea here is that you just hate actually choosing something that doesn't work out. Sticking with the default, even if it doesn't work out, is rationalized differently, even if there is no concrete reason for making a distinction between action and inaction.

A fourth explanation involves the concept of *procrastination*. You have the intention of switching away from the default, but you always put it off just a little longer until eventually you have put it off for good. A related concept involves *lethargy*. You haven't really considered the default or the alternative, and you just don't want to because it requires energy to do so. In all, regardless of why people tend to stick with defaults (and there are other explanations), this tendency can be taken advantage of by policy officials. This is the whole idea behind presumed consent in organ donation. Make being a donor the default, and more people will be donors, for whatever reason they stick with the default.

This leads us now to the empirical question: Does presumed consent increase the supply of transplantable organs? One economic study finds that cadaveric donation rates are approximately 25 percent to 30 percent higher in presumed consent countries, suggesting that defaults do have an impact on increasing the supply of organs. From a commonsense point of view, this result doesn't seem surprising. Unless defaults do not matter at all, which is unlikely, presumed consent must lead to a greater number of people designated as organ donors. However, many studies find only a modest increase in the supply of transplantable organs, and this has to do with an institutional issue that presumed consent does not address. It is very common when it is time to actually harvest organs that doctors look to the family members for explicit consent, regardless of the default. In theory, presumed consent should imply that the recently deceased individual is an organ donor, period. But if the medical practice is to still seek permission from grieving family members, and this permission is often not given, presumed consent loses its impact.

The goal of presumed consent is a noble one—to save lives. It may be uncomfortable for some to think that the government is taking advantage of the tendency of people not to take explicit actions, but setting *any* default is still a government action. The current system of donation entails a default dictated by state policy, and it has its costs and benefits. Cass Sunstein survived the criticisms he faced and was appointed to head the OIRA. I, on the other hand, have no political ambitions, so I am now going to offer a proposal that, if I was someone important, would upset people.

LEGALIZED ORGAN SNATCHING

To help alleviate the organ shortage, I want to examine a policy option that has as its single goal the maximization of the supply of cadaveric organs available for transplant. I am not claiming that this policy option is in any sense the correct one, or even that I personally endorse it. I just want to present it is a way to discuss the trade-offs associated with organ transplant policy. So what is this policy option? It is nothing less than the forced conscription of all available organs from the recently deceased.

Before you label me a complete nut for suggesting the widespread practice of the state allowing the medical profession to remove organs from the dead, I'll give you the opportunity to label me a complete nut for believing that theft in almost any context can be economically efficient. Let's return to the used-car example introduced earlier in this chapter. If I value my car at $3,000 and a potential buyer values it at $3,500, we can exploit gains from trade and negotiate a deal that moves the car from me to the buyer. The gains from trade to both parties involved in a transaction allow a market to transfer a resource to a higher-valued use, and a resource will only be transferred if the buyer's value outweighs the seller's value. A market, however, is still simply a means to an end, with the end being the efficient allocation of resources.

While it can be argued that a market is the best way to allocate resources, the existence of a market is not required to move resources to a higher-valued use. For example, if instead of buying the car, what if the buyer steals the car from me? In terms of the objective of moving the resource to its highest-valued use, stealing the car achieves the same efficient allocation of resources as does selling the car. So, why should we care *how* the resource is allocated to its highest-valued use as long as it *is* allocated to its highest-valued use?

It doesn't take much imagination to quickly point out some of the shortcomings of the efficient-theft theory. First, how can it be guaranteed that the theft will always move the resource to a higher-valued use instead of a lower-valued use? What if the person who values my car at $2,500 steals it? Second, with legalized theft, individuals are likely to underinvest in property. If I believe my car can legally be stolen at any time, I am not going to be enthusiastic about buying a car in the first place. I'd probably just steal one. Third, individuals are likely to overinvest in resources used to prevent theft, such as locks, alarms, and high-powered rifles. Finally, living in a society where your property can legally be taken from you at any time will undoubtedly upset many people. This is of no small concern. An argument of public outrage against a system of allocating resources may indeed be enough to rule out that system from serious policy consideration.

However, these arguments against stealing may have less impact when considering organ conscription. First, while it is not always the case (such as with religious objections), it is likely that far more often than not organs will be of higher-valued use if harvested for potential transplants than they will be if left with the cadaver. This, however, is a sticky point. The great advantage of a market is that the transacting individuals decide for themselves what their values are and whether there are gains from trade to be exploited. A strong criticism of nonmarket transactions is that they require a third party to decide where resources are best allocated, and that decision may be incorrect. A market transaction cannot move a resource to a lower-valued use, but a nonmarket transaction can.

Second, because you are born with your organs, underinvesting in organs is not likely to be a great concern. Of course, to dissuade the system from harvesting your organs upon death, you may decide to abuse them while alive. But choosing to take poor care of yourself *specifically* to depreciate the value of your organs is unlikely to be a serious problem. Third, overinvesting in theft protection is also not likely to be relevant. Granted, you could try to arrange to die in secret so that your organs cannot be harvested, but this behavior would occur far too infrequently to have much of an effect on the supply of organs. Finally, what about the public outrage of organ conscription? When there is a mention of some form of organ conscription in the literature, it is largely ignored due to the belief that there would be a substantial public outcry against organs being harvest without the consent of the deceased or the next of kin. One cannot argue that this outrage would not exist, but one can argue that this outrage could be offset by the benefits of conscription.

The obvious substantial advantage of organ conscription is that it will maximize the pool of available cadaveric organs for transplant. Although every organ transplantation policy has as its goal the elimination of the shortage, no reform other than conscription allows for the possibility of harvesting organs from *every* recently deceased individual. Supporters of the market solution, for example, argue that the shortage will eventually be eliminated through the pricing process. But the downside of a market solution is that, at times, the movement of a resource to a higher-valued use may *not* occur. Market transactions are not costless, and these costs may prevent the movement of a resource from a lower-valued use to a higher-valued use. If the cost of using the market prevents the exploitation of gains from trade, there is a justification for circumventing the market with some other mechanism, such as conscription.

Thus, if you are interested in allocating resources to their highest-valued use, any mechanism you propose to achieve that goal must confront two potential problems: (1) a resource that has a higher-valued use elsewhere may not be transferred, and (2) a resource may be transferred to a lower-valued use. In both cases, the value of the resource is not maximized. A market for organs, for example, avoids problem 2 but may not avoid problem 1. Conscription, on the other hand, avoids problem 1 but may not avoid problem 2. So, which is the more serious problem—too few efficient transfers or too many inefficient transfers?

If the ultimate goal is to greatly reduce the organ shortage, not transferring resources may be the more serious problem. But any policy suggestion that increases the supply of organs may be effective, so it boils down to how different policies compare empirically and what other policy goals may be of concern. Conscription, however, will provide the greatest supply of cadaveric organs compared to other policies. Furthermore, conscription may not be needed as a long-term solution. If the organ shortage can be greatly reduced, conscription can be replaced with any number of different policies that may provide a better long-term solution to prevent future shortages. And as medical technology in the transplant field continues to advance, fewer organs will be needed to maintain an adequate supply. If the current shortage of organs can be thought of as a national emergency, conscription can be thought of as an extreme, but effective, immediate solution, just as military conscription is often thought of as sound social policy in times of war.

But what about the economic downside of organ conscription— the possible transfer of resources to a lower-valued use? Just because you or I believe that, far more often than not, organ conscription will transfer resources to a higher-valued use, it is not what we believe that ultimately matters. Value is a subjective concept, and for whatever reason, organs may be more highly valued with the deceased than with a potential transfer patient. Keep in mind, however, that organs will not be harvested at the whim of the medical profession— they will be harvested to save lives.

When I teach about the different proposals to alleviate the shortage of organs available for transplant, I always ask my students to vote on which proposal they prefer. Before they vote, I offer a description of each proposal, but I don't present a detailed discussion of their relative costs and benefits. Presumed consent is usually the most preferred, establishing a market receives moderate support, and forced conscription receives no support at all. This is why I enjoy arguing in favor of conscription, to convince my students that with economic reasoning *any* policy proposal can be shown to have advantages (and disadvantages) relative to other proposals. Forced organ conscription is unlikely ever to be considered sound social policy, and possibly rightly so, but it presents an intriguing example of how an extreme short-term solution to an extreme problem need not be considered completely outrageous.

ECONOMISTS CAN SAVE LIVES—REALLY!

As severe as it seems to suggest such policy options as presumed consent or forced conscription to alleviate the organ shortage problem, allowing organs to be thought of as nothing more than property to be haggled over like used cars seems to be especially repugnant to many. Even with the concept of gains from trade assuring that *both* sides to any market transaction must benefit, certain markets (both legal and illegal) are not seen as fit places for humans to interact. Transactions involving such activities as prostitution, pornography, gambling, ticket scalping, eating horse or dog meat, smoking methamphetamine, using performance-enhancing drugs in sports, and so on, don't sit well with a great number of people. But how do economists approach the issue of repugnance over certain market transactions?

While I can't confidently speak for all economists, I do know that gains from trade is one of the fundamental tenets of economic analysis. As such, my guess is that many economists simply ignore the concept of repugnance as an argument against markets, especially from a social policy standpoint. Let's leave consenting adults to transact in peace, as long as they are not harming others. But a transaction seen as repugnant may indeed be harming others, just not in a physical way. Repugnance is more of a *psychic* cost.

Other economists, myself included, recognize that repugnance may be a true cost but shrug our shoulders as to what to do about it. Repugnance is very difficult to quantify. Furthermore, it may be difficult to even identify. You can observe a physical cost such as secondhand smoke blown in someone's face, but how do you observe someone's repugnance over the eating of horse meat? Sure, people can complain loudly about such behavior, but they must self-identify themselves. Being physically bothered by some activity, however, can be identified by others, and that may make it less difficult to implement public policy when desired. Furthermore, repugnance is usually found on both sides of the same coin. You may find it repugnant to allow for the sale of kidneys. Someone else, however, may find it repugnant that people die because they lack the opportunity to purchase a kidney. Repugnance may be a real phenomenon, but it is also a highly complicated one to deal with in any social policy debate.

Then there are some economists who cleverly put a whole new twist on the issue. In a sense, they use the concept of repugnance as their muse to develop alternative ways to reallocate resources. If the goal is to alleviate the organ shortage, yet the most discussed options are considered by many to be repugnant, can we develop other options that will be more widely accepted? The answer is yes, and one of the options is known as *kidney exchange*, and it is one of those "why didn't I think of that" ideas.

Let's say Dick and Jane are married, and Jane needs a kidney transplant. Dick would happily donate a kidney to her, so she doesn't have to be put on a waiting list, but he is not compatible with her. Bob and Sue are another married couple, and Sue needs a kidney transplant, but Bob is not compatible with her. However, it turns out that Dick is compatible with Sue, and Bob is compatible with Jane, so the four of them get together and have a four-way kidney exchange. No one has to worry about failing health while on a waiting list for a compatible kidney.

As simple as this sounds, there are some complications. One issue has to do with guaranteeing that both transplants actually occur. For example, Dick and Sue have completed their exchange, and now it is Bob's turn to donate his kidney to Jane. But Bob gets sick or has an accident that delays his surgery, or even more troubling, Bob simply changes his mind. Even if Bob is genuinely sincere in trying to donate his kidney to Jane, circumstances may prevent it. If this happens, Bob's wife has a new kidney, but Jane is out of luck, at least for now, and her husband Dick no longer has a kidney to donate through another exchange. The way around this problem is to perform the transplant surgeries *simultaneously*. All four individuals are on operating tables at the same time, and immediately after the two kidneys are removed, they are transplanted into their recipients. While this nicely solves the incentive problem, it introduces another problem—it may be costly, especially in terms of surgical space, to perform four simultaneous operations.

Another complication is in finding exactly two pairs of people compatible for the exchange. What if Dick is compatible with Sue, but Bob is not compatible with Jane? Well, kidney exchange does not have to stop with a four-way exchange. How about a six-way exchange? Let's bring in Cal and Grace. Grace needs a kidney, and Cal is not compatible with her, but he is compatible with Jane, while Bob is compatible with Grace. So, Dick donates to Sue, Bob donates to Grace, and Cal donates to Jane. Phew. Any two pairs would not be able to do a compatible kidney exchange, but all three pairs together work fine. This does exacerbate the simultaneous surgery problem, but it also allows for more life-saving kidney transplants.

Developing the algorithms necessary to facilitate kidney exchanges can be a daunting task, especially because the success of the program depends on the size of the patient-donor database. The more people in the database the better, but the more difficult it becomes to organize exchanges. There are also several key issues the algorithms may take into account. Kidney exchange compatibility is not just a yes-or-no proposition, but instead there are degrees of compatibility that need to be matched carefully. Also, can you accommodate a donor-recipient pair in which only one of them is currently matched with someone else in the program? As a greater number of exchanges at one time are considered, can the surgeries be performed nonsimultaneously? The key point is that it can be very complicated to organize and operate a kidney exchange program.

So what does all this have to do with economics? Harvard economist Al Roth has been a pioneer in the development of the algorithms necessary to develop a well-functioning and complex kidney exchange program. His research has been extremely influential in this field, and he continues to be involved in improving the program. As a measure of the success of the program, in 2009 two 12-paired exchanges and one 13-paired exchange took place, each exchange involving multiple hospitals. That's a total of 37 people receiving kidney transplants in just three exchanges. Whether the exchange program can continue to grow in a way that will put a serious dent in the organ shortage problem remains to be seen, but it is a clever and impressive start. And most importantly, no one seems to find it repugnant. Economists are saving lives. Who would believe?

NOTES

The citations for the two appeals for the Moore case are Moore v. The Regents of the University of California, 249 Cal. Rptr. 494 (1988); and Moore v. The Regents of the University of California, 271 Cal. Rptr. 146 (1990).

The basic idea for the result that a resource will move to its highest-valued use as long as a property right is assigned to either party can be attributed to Ronald Coase. See his article "The Problem of Social Cost," *Journal of Law and Economics* 3 (1960): 1–44. For a more accessible discussion, see any textbook in law and economics, such as Richard A. Posner's *Economic Analysis of Law*, 3rd ed. (Boston: Little, Brown, 1986).

The article on pricing a kidney is by Gary S. Becker and Julio Jorge Elias, "Introducing Incentives in the Market for Live and Cadaveric Organ Donations," *Journal of Economic Perspectives* 21 (2007): 3–24. Other articles discussing a market for organs are by David H. Howard, "Producing Organ Donors," *Journal of Economic Perspectives* 21 (2007): 25–36; and William Barnett II, Michael Saliba, and Deborah Walker, "A Free Market in Kidneys: Efficient and Equitable," *Independent Review* 5 (2001): 373–85.

A discussion of defaults and the status quo bias can be found in Colin Camerer et al., "Regulation for Conservatives: Behavioral Economics and the Case for 'Asymmetric Paternalism,'" *University of Pennsylvania Law Review* 151 (2003): 1211–54.

The ability of presumed consent to increase the amount of organs available for transplant is discussed by Alberto Abadie and Sebastien Gay, "The Impact of Presumed Consent

Legislation on Cadaveric Organ Donation: A Cross-Country Study," *Journal of Health Economics* 25 (2006): 599–620; and Eric J. Johnson and Daniel Goldstein, "Do Defaults Save Lives?" *Science* 302 (2003): 1338–39.

A sample of the research on kidney exchanges by Alvin Roth and his colleagues can be found in the following articles: Alvin E. Roth, Tayfun Sonmez, and M. Utku Unver, "Kidney Exchange," *Quarterly Journal of Economics* 119 (2004): 457–88; Alvin E. Roth, Tayfun Sonmez, and M. Utku Unver, "A Kidney Exchange Clearinghouse in New England," *AEA Papers and Proceedings* 95 (2005): 376–380; and Alvin E. Roth, "Repugnance as a Constraint on Markets," *Journal of Economic Perspectives* 21 (2007): 37–58. Also see the article by Virginia Postrel, "With Functioning Kidneys for All," *Atlantic*, July 2009 (unbound), 1–10.

For an excellent collection of readings that cover virtually every aspect of the debate on organ transplants, see Arthur L. Caplan and Daniel H. Coello, *The Ethics of Organ Transplants: The Current Debate* (Amherst, NY: Prometheus Books, 1998).

4 What's Yours Is Mine

A WHILE BACK, I went to see a movie. When the lights went down, the first image that came up on the screen was that of a man in a baseball cap. He was a movie set painter, and he talked about several of the movies he had worked on. As the short piece progressed, its purpose became clear—it was a heartfelt plea against movie piracy. Unfortunately, seconds after the plea ended, a trailer for *Jeepers Creepers 2* (about a winged man/beast trying to eat a busload of high school students) distracted the audience from breaking up into small discussion groups to further consider the piracy issue. However, I did take note of a website address that I was able to check out the next day.

Under the heading "Why Should I Care?" the website offered four concise reasons as to why I should not pirate movies:

1. *You're cheating yourself.* The more I pirate movies, the more difficult it will be for the movie studios to recoup their investment, and fewer movies will be produced for my future enjoyment.
2. *You're threatening the livelihood of thousands.* The entertainment industry is made up not only of big stars and directors but also of over 500,000 everyday working people (like the above-mentioned set painter). If fewer movies are produced, many of these people will lose their jobs.
3. *Your computer is vulnerable.* File-sharing computer sites open my computer up to destructive viruses and worms.

4. *You're breaking the law.* Downloading copyrighted movies off the Internet is illegal, and it is not difficult for investigators to trace this illegal activity back to my computer. If I am caught, it is possible that I can lose my job, face up to five years in prison, and face up to $250,000 in fines.

It is not difficult to appreciate why movie producers are upset with movie piracy. The more pirated movies that are distributed, the less revenue there will be for movie producers to enjoy. I may be cheating myself if I pirate movies, but I assure you that movie producers are far more concerned with me cheating *them*. What may be more difficult to appreciate, however, is that movie piracy, or copyright infringement in general, may be economically efficient. Then again, it may not be.

A PRIMER ON PRICING

To thoroughly discuss the trade-offs associated with copyright or patent law, I really should be drawing graphs. But this book is going to be 100 percent graph free, or your money back. Instead, I will use words to explain how, according to economic theory, a firm determines the price of its product. There are three main factors that *simultaneously* determine a firm's price.

Demand: The Consumer's Willingness to Pay for the Product

As I discussed in the previous chapter, the maximum amount a consumer is willing to pay for a product determines the consumer's *value* for that product. The more a consumer is willing to pay for a unit of the product, the higher the product price may be.

Supply: The Costs of Production

For gains from trade to exist, the maximum amount a consumer is willing to pay for a product must exceed the minimum amount a firm needs to be willing to sell the product. Generally, a firm needs to at least cover its costs of production to reap gains from trade of a sale. Unfortunately, a comprehensive discussion of the different types of costs of production and how they affect price will have most readers quickly flipping ahead to the next chapter. Instead, I will use a simple hypothetical example and boil things down to just two key concepts—*up-front* costs and *incremental* costs.

Suppose you are a book publisher and you decide to buy a book from an author. If you make a one-time payment to the author for publishing rights, that payment can be considered an up-front cost. In other words, before you even produce one copy of the book, you have already incurred a cost that is now behind you. Ahead of you are the incremental costs of publishing the book, that is, the costs you have to incur to physically produce individual units of the book. These costs will include paper costs, printing costs, possibly marketing and distribution costs, and so forth. For each unit of the book you decide to produce, you must, at a minimum, expect to set a price that covers the incremental cost. The greater you can set the price above the incremental cost, the more gains from trade per unit you can receive. But to decide to purchase the publishing rights in the first place, you must set a price that ultimately will return enough revenue to you to also cover your up-front cost.

Market Structure: The Number of Competing Firms

In general, the more firms there are producing an identical (or very similar) product, the lower the price will be. Firms that don't offer a competitive price can be undercut by their rivals. If there is only one firm producing a product, that firm is referred to as a *monopoly*. Monopoly pricing generally yields the highest price relative to the price from any other market structure.

In a competitive market where there are many firms, price is usually driven down close to the incremental cost of production. For example, assume that as soon as you publish your book and offer it for sale, other firms can use the exact same text and publish their own copies of the book. Because they didn't have to incur the up-front cost that you incurred, the minimum price they can set only has to cover the incremental cost. If, however, you are a monopolist, by definition you face no competitors. Thus, a monopolist can set a price above the incremental cost and earn a per unit profit without fear of a rival undercutting that price.

A monopolist's best price is one that yields the maximum profit. This implies that a monopolist must be concerned with setting too low a price *or* too high a price. Compared to the profit maximizing price, at a lower price a monopolist sells more units but at a smaller price-cost margin per unit. At a higher price, a monopolist has a higher price-cost margin per unit but sells fewer units. Thus, even a monopolist must be concerned with demand and cost conditions in determining a product's best price.

COPYRIGHT PROTECTION: A CLASSIC TRADE-OFF

Copyright protection assigns exclusive rights over the sale and distribution of intellectual property to the owner of that property. If you are a book publisher, copyright protection, in effect, gives you monopoly power in the selling of your product. Copyright protection leads to a classic economic trade-off. The benefit of the protection is that it can provide incentives for creators of intellectual property to continue to create. The cost of the protection is that it can lead to monopoly pricing in the selling of the property.

As I discussed above, if you are a book publisher, you ultimately have to earn enough revenue to cover all your costs. Without copyright protection, it is possible that as soon as you release your book, other firms will immediately copy and sell it. These copying firms are likely to be able to undercut your price, because they do not have to be compensated for the same type of up-front costs that you incurred. If you are farsighted, before you ever purchase the publishing rights for the book, you will look ahead and anticipate the problem of not being able to ultimately cover your up-front costs. At that early stage, without copyright protection you may decide not to purchase the publishing rights from the author. If this were true for every book publisher, the author would not be compensated and, therefore, may decide not to write the book in the first place. Thus, some argue, copyright protection is necessary to maintain a sufficient level of valuable intellectual property.

The downside of copyright protection is that it creates monopoly power. Assuming that the copyright protection can be enforced, you are now the only one who can legally sell the book (or allow others to sell the book for you). With monopoly power comes monopoly pricing, and that can reduce *social* welfare. But exactly why monopoly pricing reduces social welfare is the important issue.

If I decide to pay $25 for the new Harry Potter book, that implies that I value the book at a minimum of $25. Certainly, I'd like to pay as little as possible for the book. The less I pay the more gains from trade I get. But if I actually purchase the book, I must be getting some gains from trade. On the other hand, if you value the book less than $25, you won't buy it, because you wouldn't realize any gains from trade from the transaction. Thus, there are two types of consumers we have to distinguish between: those who purchase the product at the monopoly price and those who don't.

If I purchase the book at the monopoly price, I am not reducing social welfare. As discussed in the previous chapter, it is the realization of gains from trade that is important for economic efficiency, not how the gains are shared. By raising the price above the incremental cost, a firm with monopoly power simply has the ability to reap more gains from trade than a competitive firm. What is important in maximizing social welfare is that a purchase is made by every consumer who values the book more than the minimum amount at which the firm is willing to sell it. That is, social welfare is maximized when all potential gains from trade in a market are realized. With monopoly power, this won't occur.

As discussed above, competitive firms generally compete price down close to the incremental cost of producing a unit of the product. If the incremental cost is the minimum amount a firm needs to cover, gains from trade exist for every consumer who values the product more than the incremental cost. (Consumers who value the book *less* than the incremental cost are properly excluded from the market, as there are no gains from trade selling to them.) Thus, in a competitive market, price competition allows for the realization of all gains from trade possible in that market, even though the consumers reap all the gains from trade and the firms reap none. By raising price above the incremental cost, a monopolist creates a gap between the price of the product and the minimum amount needed to produce the product. If a consumer's willingness to pay falls within this gap, there are gains from trade that will not be realized because the price is too high. This loss in gains from trade is the social cost of monopoly power.

DO WE NEED PROTECTION?

The key social argument in favor of copyright protection is that it provides incentives for the creation of intellectual property. But copyright protection is not the only means of providing such incentives. Several factors influence the creation of intellectual property, and if these factors are effective, they can weaken the argument in favor of copyright protection. These other factors include

Poor quality of copies. If poor copying technology leads to copies that are inferior to the original, copying will not be a perfect substitute for the original. Even if the quality of the copies is high, many consumers may still prefer to purchase the original product.

Copying takes time. Because the original producer will be the first to the market, there will be a time lag that can be exploited before copying can take place. This time lag may be enough for the original producer to recoup the up-front cost, and then some.

High production costs of copies. It is possible that the incremental costs of copying are fairly high, not only compared to the cost of producing the original, but also compared to the price of purchasing the original. Furthermore, even though it is likely that the copier has fewer up-front costs than the original producer, there may still be up-front costs of copying. These costs make it more difficult to produce copies.

Copying may enhance the value of the original product. It is possible that a consumer's willingness to pay for a product *depends* on the consumer's ability to make copies. For example, libraries subscribe to academic journals and provide photocopy machines for their patrons to use. Without the photocopying technology, patrons may be less interested in the journals, and the libraries may be less interested in subscribing to them. If this is the case, the demand for the journal subscription depends on the availability of the copying technology. This enhanced demand can lead to a higher price being set.

Nonfinancial motives for creating intellectual property. Many authors and artists create intellectual property for the joy of being creative. Furthermore, the funding needed to create intellectual property may come from sources other than eventual sales, such as family support, private donations, or public subsidies.

Taken together, these factors can determine whether copyright protection is necessary to encourage the creation of intellectual property. The legal battle between music companies and Napster over Napster's music file-sharing technology, a battle Napster lost, provides an excellent setting in which to illustrate many of these factors.

First, music companies do enjoy some lag time before copying can take place, although that lag time may be very short. In any event, there are still many consumers who prefer the original product. Second, Napster has argued that the file-sharing technology actually enhances the demand for the original product. Potential consumers can sample different songs to determine which compact discs they would like to purchase. Furthermore, even if the original product is not purchased, file sharing can greatly enhance the demand for live performances and promotional merchandise. Third, it is argued that the vast majority of musicians do not reap much of a financial gain from creating music. For every commercially successful band, there are possibly hundreds of local bands that play music for the love of playing music. There is simply too much music produced for the file sharing to have any significant impact in reducing the quantity or quality of music creation.

Although at this point it sounds like I've been hired by Napster to defend its actions, I will now turn to the (inevitable) other side of the story. The strongest argument in favor of copyright enforcement against file sharing has to do with the low cost of producing copies. I remember when the music industry was terrified of the blank audio cassette, just as the film and television industries were terrified of the blank video cassette. Can you imagine how these industries must feel about digital copying technology? Although there is an up-front cost to purchasing the necessary equipment to share digital files, computers have become extremely commonplace. Not only are computers now fairly affordable, they have many uses well beyond music file sharing. As for the incremental cost of making copies, this is now negligible. It is inexpensive and technically simple for anyone with a computer to access the Internet to participate in music file sharing. All it takes is one person to make available a file that literally millions of other people can share. Furthermore, while audiophiles may disagree, the average listener tends to find little difference in sound quality between the copy and the original. And as the technology rapidly improves, so will the sound quality of the copy. These arguments suggest that without copyright protection, the music industry may be substantially harmed by file-sharing technology, and this may reduce the quantity and quality of music creation.

Not long after the Napster case, the Supreme Court considered the issue of music file sharing with the Grokster case. The Grokster case differentiated itself from Napster due to an interesting fact— Grokster itself did not store any music files on its servers and, therefore, could not be considered *direct* copyright infringers. Grokster provided software, free of charge, that greatly facilitated file sharing across users. No information needed to pass through any computers owned or controlled by Grokster. With Napster, when users searched for files, the information passed through Napster's central servers. Furthermore, Napster's central server maintained an index of users and files available on the network. So, simply put, if Grokster shut down its computers, that would have no impact on the file sharing ability of the users. If Napster shut down its computers, file sharing would be halted.

So why was Grokster on the chopping block for copyright infringement if it did not infringe? Grokster was considered a *contributory infringer*. It did not infringe, but it made it easier for others to infringe. Contributory infringement must strike a delicate balance between legal uses and illegal uses. As an illustrative example, consider the locksmith tools industry. With a quick search online, I found the following advertisement for a lockpick tool known as the Kwick Pick:

Locked out? Now you can open virtually any lock in just seconds with Kwick Pick! Professional-quality Dyno Kwick Lock Pick gets you in—in a flash! The Kwick Pick fits comfortably in your hand, and opens everything from padlocks to file cabinets, from desk drawers to toolboxes, from luggage to gas caps. Kwick Pick even opens some car doors and front door locks. . . . The Dyno Kwick Pick was invented by a professional locksmith. . . . Don't know how to pick a lock? This is a great little tool to have around the house or office! With the Dyno Kwick lock pick tool you don't need to know how to pick locks. Naturally, your Kwick Pick comes with full instructions. . . . The Dyno Kwick Pick is the perfect stocking-stuffer for the guy that has everything.

The company may not be directly advertising to criminals, but it's not a big stretch to believe that this handy tool can find its way into the hands of those who would use it for illegal purposes. But there are legal uses for a lockpick, and those uses are what allow a product like the Kwick Pick to be openly sold. I, however, asked my wife to buy me a different stocking stuffer advertised on the website—the Handcuff Shim Pick. You just never know when that will come in handy.

In the Grokster case, its software allowed users to share files with amazing efficiency. And even though there are legal uses for such software, such as sharing noncopyrighted material or using it for nonsharing purposes, the potential for illegal sharing was tremendous. In the court's view, the balance was not difficult to measure, as it found the potential for illegal file sharing with the Grokster software to be on too large a scale to be declared noninfringing. Grokster was shut down.

As a brief conclusion to the Grokster case, in reaching its decision the Supreme Court made note of a couple of issues that it felt exacerbated the contributory infringement. While Grokster provided the software for free, it made revenue by directly streaming advertisements to its users. Also, Grokster was fully aware that users were using the software for copyright infringement purposes, and there was evidence that supported the fact that Grokster *intended* its software to be used for illegal infringing. Analysts of the Grokster decision have differing opinions as to whether the court would have found against Grokster if not for these aggravating issues. From an economic perspective, however, Grokster's knowledge of the illegal uses, or its indirect profiting from such use, is not likely to be a key issue. Most importantly, the social cost of Grokster's software is its potentially adverse impact on the creation of intellectual property and the impact on the music industry.

The above discussion only deals with the issue of whether copyright protection is necessary to encourage the creation of intellectual property. If it isn't necessary, that eliminates the main argument in favor of copyright. But even if it is necessary, that still doesn't deal with the main cost of copyright protection: the creation of monopoly power. The argument for or against copyright, however, does not have to be absolute. There is a legal gray area that allows for copyright protection *and* legalized copying.

IS IT EFFICIENT TO BE FAIR?

Consider the facts of the following case, based on a real-world case from the early 1970s. A United States government library subscribed to several medical journals and provided free photocopies of articles in these journals to other libraries, government agencies, and commercial organizations. Thousands of photocopies were made and distributed. The publisher of the journals claimed that its copyrights were being infringed, and it filed a lawsuit against the government. The government's defense was that it was not infringing on copyrighted work, because the copying was legally protected by a doctrine known as *fair use*.

Fair use allows an individual to legally copy copyrighted work. There are several factors that the courts consider in determining whether the copying can be considered fair use:

1. The purpose and character of the use, including whether such use is of a commercial nature or is for nonprofit educational purposes.
2. The nature of the copyrighted work.
3. The amount and substantiality of the portion used in relation to the copyrighted work as a whole.
4. The effect of the use upon the potential market for or value of the copyrighted work.

The economic rationale for fair use is similar to the rationale for organ conscription that I presented in the previous chapter. Fair use can facilitate the movement of a resource, or more accurately a copy of the resource, from one party to another. In the organ transplant example, there exists no current market mechanism for moving a resource from one use to another, and conscription is presented as an *alternative* to a possible market solution. In contrast, the sole purpose of fair use is to allow copies to *circumvent* an existing market mechanism.

As discussed in the previous chapter, a downside of the market solution is that it may prevent the movement of a resource to a higher-valued use if there is an imperfection in the market mechanism. In the case of copyright, one such mechanism may be the firm's ability to set a monopoly price and exclude certain consumers from the market. This creates a loss in gains from trade. By allowing these consumers to take advantage of the fair use doctrine, the courts, in effect, are undercutting the firm's monopoly power. Consumers who would purchase the good at a competitive price, but not at a monopoly price, can now copy the good without infringing on the firm's copyright. This is a strong economic rationale for fair use.

Another possible market imperfection, also discussed in the previous chapter, is the existence of transactions costs. If it is too costly for some consumers to transact with the firm, gains from trade may not be exploited. Fair use allows these consumers to circumvent the transactions process, thus allowing the resource to move to a higher-valued use. The transaction-cost rationale for fair use is often presented by economists. The question raised is this: If there were a perfectly working market, how would resources be allocated? If this question can be answered, the next step is to impose some alternative to the market solution to try to mimic the outcome of the hypothetical market with no imperfections. Fair use is one such alternative.

In the library case, it may be that the monopoly subscription price for the medical journal was too high for some individuals to subscribe. Alternatively, some individuals may have only valued an article or two, as opposed to a whole subscription. However, transactions costs may have been too high to allow the publisher to transact with individuals for specific articles. The court did consider whether some market solution could be set up in which the publisher could sell individual copies, but the majority opinion did not believe such a market could exist. The court reasoned that if certain individuals were excluded from the market, fair use would allow these individuals to get copies of the articles through a nonmarket mechanism. But this raises an interesting question: If fair use only allows *noncustomers* to get copies of the firm's product, why would any firm ever challenge fair use in court? It wouldn't be losing customers, so why would it care?

In practice, it is very difficult to apply the fair use doctrine to a narrow category of users. A rule that allows only noncustomers fair use, but excludes current customers, would be difficult to enforce. In this case, fair use may allow some current customers to become current copiers instead, and this will negatively impact the firm's revenues. Furthermore, the easier it is to make copies, the easier it is to *sell* the copies, and this can further compete away current customers who may not have access to the copying technologies themselves. This is why the factors the courts consider in adopting fair use include whether the copying will have a commercial use and whether the firm would be too adversely affected by the copying. But even if the courts explicitly take into account the possible adverse effect of fair use on the firm, the courts and the firm may disagree as to the extent of the adverse effect. This usually explains why firms challenge the doctrine of fair use even if, in theory, it can be applied in a way that doesn't harm them.

In the real medical journal case, the court allowed the copying to be considered fair use by applying the four factors listed above. Access to medical research through academic journal articles was considered to be extremely valuable not only to the copiers but ultimately to the public through whatever gains future research would yield. Although many users of the copies would ultimately commercially gain from the research, the copies themselves were not being directly used for commercial gain. Furthermore, although the total amount of copying was immense, the government library did place certain restrictions on individual requests for copies, since it was more difficult to get a copy of a recently published article. Finally, the court did not feel that the publisher was adversely affected by the copying. Because of the self-imposed restrictions the library placed on the copy requests, and because many requests were for back issues that were not readily available from the publisher, the court decided that fair use would not greatly reduce the value of the copyright to the publisher.

It should be noted that fair use is not only granted for "educational" uses. When the blank video cassette was introduced, Universal City Studios and Walt Disney Productions sued Sony Corporation, the manufacturer of video cassette recorders. The Supreme Court ruled that home copying of television shows for later viewing (called *time-shifting*) did not substantially harm the studios, and videotaping was considered fair use. Napster and Grokster, however, did not do as well in arguing that file sharing constituted fair use. Even if the file sharing was for personal use, there was a belief that the copies would be substitutes for compact disc purchases, and the music companies would be substantially harmed through lost sales.

ARE PHARMACEUTICAL COMPANIES GREEDY?
OF COURSE, THANKFULLY

As intense is the debate over copyright protection for books and music, patent protection for (legal) drugs is even more intense. A high price on a book or a compact disc may reduce gains from trade over entertainment products, but a high price on a life-saving prescription drug may lead to a loss in lives. The trade-offs associated with patent protection mirror those associated with copyright protection, so I will only briefly consider patents. But as I discussed in the last chapter, health issues and profit motives don't mix well for many people. Even in the medical journal copyright case, because the copies were used for medical research, the fair use exception to copyright protection was easy for the court to rationalize. Had the library been distributing copies of articles from entertainment magazines, the fair use exception may have been a much tougher sale.

Let's start with the factors that determine a pharmaceutical firm's price for its products. On the demand side, there are several factors that can lead to a high price. First, the decision to purchase a drug may not be made by the consumer of the product, but instead it is often made by a physician. This reduces the importance of price in the consumer's purchase decision. Second, because drugs are used to combat illnesses, the willingness to pay tends to be high. Finally, many consumers have their drug purchases subsidized by insurance plans. To the extent that a consumer doesn't bear the full cost of the drug, the price can be higher.

On the supply side, the cost structure for drug production is similar to what I discussed above: the up-front costs and incremental costs. In the case of pharmaceuticals, however, the up-front costs can be phenomenal. It is not uncommon for it to cost hundreds of millions of dollars and to take up to 12 years to bring a new drug to the market. The up-front costs include the discovery and development of a new drug. A firm wishing to introduce a new drug in the US market must demonstrate both the safety and efficacy of the drug to the Food and Drug Administration (FDA). The testing procedures, initially with animals and then with a small number of human volunteers working up to a larger number, are rigorous and make up much of the up-front costs. The incremental costs of drug production, on the other hand, are generally quite modest.

One economic study, using a sample of 68 drugs drawn from 10 pharmaceutical companies, estimates that the average out-of-pocket cost of developing a new drug is $403 million (in 2000 dollars), and it takes approximately eight years to go from the initial development stage to marketing approval. In addition, the authors estimate the opportunity cost of the out-of-pocket costs over the eight years to be $399 million. This leads them to conclude that the average cost of developing and bringing a new drug to the market is $802 million. This figure was widely publicized in the media, and it drew much criticism. Questions were raised about the sample of drugs used and the way many out-of-pocket costs were estimated. No one doubts that it is very costly to develop new drugs, but there is a legitimate debate over the magnitude of these costs.

There is also criticism over the authors' use of opportunity costs in their estimate. For example, one critic of the authors' estimate, (a former editor in chief of the prestigious *New England Journal of Medicine*), puts it this way:

The authors justified the maneuver on the grounds that, from the perspective of investors, a pharmaceutical company is really just one kind of investment, which they choose among other possible options. But while this may be true for investors, surely it is not true for the companies themselves. The latter have no choice but to spend money on research and development if they wish to be in the pharmaceutical business. They are not investment houses. So you can hardly look at the money spent on research and development as money that could have been spent on something else. The authors say adding opportunity costs is standard accounting practice, and that may be so, but in the context of pharmaceutical research and development, it simply makes no sense.

The problem with this argument is that it suffers from a fundamental misunderstanding of the concept of opportunity cost. While it is true that a pharmaceutical company is in the business of developing and marketing drugs, there is nothing to stop that company from taking its resources and investing them in any venture it chooses. Furthermore, it can simply stop being a pharmaceutical company if it so desires. Saying that a pharmaceutical company has no opportunity costs because it chooses to be a pharmaceutical company makes no economic sense. A better criticism in this case may be to question how the authors technically estimate the opportunity cost. Economists may disagree about the magnitudes of the costs of developing a new drug, and whether patent protection is currently too generous or not generous enough, but there is little disagreement over the inclusion of opportunity costs in any legitimate cost estimate.

As with artistic intellectual property, ultimately the firm's drug price must be high enough to allow for revenue that will cover all of its costs. If a competitive market structure forces the price down close to incremental cost, the firm may not be able to recoup its up-front costs. Patent protection in this case gives the firm some monopoly power and the ability to set price above incremental cost. But, as I argued with copyright, are there alternatives to patent protection that give a pharmaceutical company the ability to cover all of its costs?

While it may be reasonable to argue that a lot of artistic intellectual property will be created by artists with motives that are not solely financial, you rarely hear that argument applied to pharmaceutical companies. Certainly, there are many medical researchers who sincerely want to improve the quality of life for millions of people, but pharmaceutical companies are primarily profit-motivated businesses. As for copying technology, a drug is a specific chemical entity that can be copied exactly. Once the molecular compound is known, a rival manufacturer can perfectly copy the drug without having to replicate any of the discovery or development procedures. It is true, however, that a new drug can be introduced into the market with a reasonable time lag before it can be copied and marketed, but will the time lag be enough to recoup twelve years of up-front costs?

Another difficulty pharmaceutical companies face is that many of the drugs they discover end up not surviving the development process or eventually not gaining FDA approval. These drugs may never be marketed, but ultimately *their* up-front costs also need to be recouped. In contrast, it may be true that many artistic projects end up not returning a profit, but most projects actually can be marketed to recoup at least part of their up-front costs.

One other problem that pharmaceutical companies must contend with is the difficulty in recouping up-front costs from sales in foreign markets. Probably the most common criticism I see concerning American pharmaceutical companies is that they set higher drug prices at home than they do abroad. This is very easy to explain. Many other countries either offer no patent protection for pharmaceutical companies or they adopt government price controls for drugs. Generic drug competition forces price down close to incremental costs, and government price controls do the same. What may be surprising, however, is that higher prices at home may be *beneficial* to Americans.

The key benefit to patent protection is that it can allow a firm to set price above its incremental cost, allowing it to recoup both incremental and up-front costs. If the United States does away with patent protection to match other countries, a pharmaceutical company may have few markets in which it can successfully recoup all of its costs. In this case, it may not be profitable to try to discover and develop new drugs. Americans may be unhappy with high drug prices, but those high prices may be the only thing spurring on new research. And it must always be remembered that the pharmaceutical industry has developed phenomenal life-improving and life-saving medications that benefit millions of people.

The flip side of the story is that the high prices can lead to the monopoly problem of having some consumers excluded from the market. It comes back to the classic trade-off: the high prices may be necessary to encourage drug production, but the high prices may also create a monopoly social loss. Furthermore, in general there are social costs to patents beyond the monopoly social loss due to high prices. Some firms seek patents not to encourage their own production but to demand licensing fees from other firms that need the patented technology in their own production. This may lead to defensive patenting, in which firms seek patents so as not to be subject to other firms' patents, creating a tremendous amount of (possibly redundant) administrative costs. In addition, new invention typically relies on older invention, and the more difficult it is for firms to acquire access to older technology because of patent protection, the more costly it will be to invent new technology.

Patent protection is not absolute. The typical effective life of a patent is around twenty years. After that, generic competitors can enter the market. The question is: Is this too much or too little patent protection? Although this question is very difficult to answer, I will leave you with the thoughts of F. M. Scherer, one of the leading economic scholars on patent protection:

> In the author's considered judgment, a pell-mell march toward regulation of pharmaceutical industry pricing could seriously impair the industry's incentives for investments in new products. Governmental bodies that regulate prices and profits characteristically have a myopic bias. They are inclined toward . . . emphasizing recapture of "excess" profits on the relatively few highly profitable products with-

out taking into account failures or limping successes experienced on the much larger number of other entries. If profits were held to "reasonable" levels on the blockbuster drugs, aggregate profits would almost surely be insufficient to sustain a high rate of technological progress. . . . Should a trade-off be required between modestly excessive prices and profits versus retarded technical progress, it would be better to err on the side of excessive profits.

NOTES

The website about copyright infringement with the section titled "Why Should I Care?" was found at http://www.respectcopyright.org.

If you are interested in a more thorough economic discussion of a firm's pricing decision, see any principles of microeconomics textbook, such as the text by Arthur O'Sullivan, Steven M. Sheffrin, and Stephen J. Perez, *Microeconomics: Principles, Applications, and Tools*, 7th ed. (Boston, MA: Prentice-Hall, 2012)

Alternatives to copyright protection are discussed in William M. Landes and Richard A. Posner, "An Economic Analysis of Copyright Law," *Journal of Legal Studies* 18 (1989): 325–63.

An interesting debate over the merits of copyright protection can be found in a series of articles in the *Review of Law and Economics*, volume 5 (2009), issue 3, including the following: Michele Boldrin and David K. Levine, "Does Intellectual Monopoly Help Innovation?," 991–1024; Charles McManis, "A Rhetorical Response to Boldrin and Levine: Against Intellectual (Property) Extremism," 1082–1100; and Liza S. Vertinsky, "Responding to the Challenges of 'Against Intellectual Monopoly,'" 1115–29.

A discussion of the economic issues in the Napster case can be found in a series of papers in the *American Economic Review*, volume 92 (May 2002). The papers are Benjamin Klein, Andres V. Lerner, and Kevin M. Murphy, "The Economics of Copyright: 'Fair Use' in a Networked World," 205–8; Michele Boldrin and David Levine, "The Case against Intellectual Property," 209–12; and Paul Romer, "When Should We Use Intellectual Property Rights?," 213–16. A nice summary of these papers is presented by Douglas Clement, "Creation Myths: Does Innovation Require Intellectual Property Rights?" *Reason Online*, March 2003.

A discussion of the Grokster case can be found on the always interesting *Becker-Posner Blog* (July 3, 2005). They also discuss pharmaceutical patents on December 12, 2004.

The factors the courts consider in fair use cases can be found at *United States Code Annotated, Title 17, Copyrights, Section 107, Limitations on Exclusive Rights: Fair Use.*

The case cited for the medical journals example is Williams and Wilkins Company v. The United States, 487 F.2d 1345 (1973). The case cited for the blank video cassette example is Sony Corp. of America v. Universal City Studios, Inc., 464 U.S. 417 (1984). The case cited for the Napster example is A&M Records, Inc. v. Napster, Inc., 114 F. Supp. 2d 896 (2000). The case cited for the Grokster example is Metro-Goldwyn-Mayer Studios, Inc. v. Grokster, Ltd., 545 U.S. 913 (2005).

Two interesting articles on fair use are by Wendy J. Gordon, "Fair Use as Market Failure: A Structural and Economic Analysis of the Betamax Case and Its Predecessors," *Columbia Law Review* 82 (1982): 1600–1657, and Cynthia M. Cimino, "Fair Use in the Digital Age: Are We Playing Fair?," *Tulane Journal of Technology and Intellectual Property* 4 (2002): 203–11.

For a general discussion of the economics of the pharmaceutical industry, see the text by W. Kip Viscusi, John M. Vernon, and Joseph E. Harrington, *Economics of Regulation and Antitrust*, 4th ed. (Cambridge, MA: MIT Press, 2005). Also see the article by Ernst R. Berndt, "Pharmaceuticals in U.S. Health Care: Determinants of Quantity and Price," *Journal of Economic Perspectives* 16 (2002): 45–66.

The quote on the questionable use of opportunity cost is by Marcia Angell, *The Truth About the Drug Companies* (New York, NY: Random House, 2005): 45.

The quote that ends the chapter is by F. M. Scherer, "Pricing, Profits, and Technological Progress in the Pharmaceutical Industry," *Journal of Economic Perspectives* 7 (1993): 113.

5 *Eat, Drink, Smoke, and Be Unhappy*

A WHILE BACK, I was playing poker at a private club with a bunch of guys who were either smoking cigarettes or complaining about those who were smoking cigarettes. The complaints were harsh. *You have to be an idiot to smoke. Is there anyone dumber than a smoker? You may as well just put a gun to your head.* This went on for a while, but when the smoke finally cleared (just a figure of speech, the cigarette smoke never actually cleared), I politely asked a simple question: What about the *benefits* of smoking? At this moment, the room fell silent and all eyes were upon me. One guy, who was giving me a cold hard stare, responded quite succinctly: There are *no* benefits to smoking.

Over the past few years, I have given many public talks on the economics of smoking, and have often heard that very response, but this time there was an important difference. The guy who said that there are no benefits to smoking was smoking a cigarette at the time. As he sat there, cigarette burning in his hand, I asked him why he smoked. He thought about it for a minute, and then, rather defensively, told me that he smoked because he enjoyed it. So I said, "Isn't enjoyment a benefit?" He continued to stare at me, and then a smile slowly appeared upon his face. He now smokes twice as much as before.

If a smoker himself has a difficult time considering the benefits of smoking, how difficult must it be for the vast majority of people who aren't smokers to think of such benefits? And policy officials, especially those concerned with health issues, must also tend to be skeptical or purposely dismissive of such benefits. Consider the opinion of two epidemiologists responding to an economist's 1995 article in *Regulation* on the benefits of smoking:

> The disease consequences of tobacco use, ultimately measured in the loss of productive human life, make up the entire risk-benefit picture, unbalanced by concrete benefits.

Smoking is an unhealthy activity, not only to the smoker but to others who are exposed to the secondhand smoke. So certainly there are costs to smoking, and it is these costs that motivate social policy intervention to reduce the incidence of smoking. But what about the benefits of smoking? It is easy to identify several benefits, the most obvious one is that smokers enjoy doing it. The more daunting task is to argue that there are no benefits to an activity that is undertaken by nearly 20 percent of the world's adult population.

As an economist, I have been trained to think of costs and benefits together. I can't even think of one term without immediately thinking of the other, even for an activity that is associated with substantial adverse health outcomes, such as smoking. But not all economists approach the issue of smoking in exactly the same way. For example, in a prestigious collection of health economics articles, the authors of a survey on the economics of smoking state the following in their objective:

> The subsequent economic analysis has been motivated by a desire to determine how economic forces influence tobacco consumption, with continued emphasis on refining the scientific rigor of the work; but the objective of much of the research is now to determine how to harness economic forces and logic, how to use economic tools, to decrease smoking, with the ultimate goal being to reduce the toll of tobacco.

And then in a footnote, they add:

Not all of the research is motivated by a desire to decrease smoking. Some authors express the opinion that more respect should be accorded consumer sovereignty, despite the issues of addiction and youthful initiation of smoking that have led many economists to perceive the market for cigarettes as suffering from important market imperfections.

Although the authors do not claim that there are no benefits to smoking, they assume that market imperfections are prevalent enough to allow their analysis to focus on the reduction of smoking as their goal. Personally, however, I would not relegate the concept of consumer sovereignty to a footnote and then abruptly dismiss it. Nor would I consider the reduction of smoking as the obvious goal of economic analysis. Instead, the goal I would consider is the maximization of social welfare, which may be a broader concept than the reduction of smoking.

It is not a difficult task to use economic reasoning to justify a reduction in or complete ban on smoking. If you believe that the costs of smoking outweigh the benefits, either due to precise scientific evidence or just because you have a gut feeling, you may believe that social welfare is maximized by banning smoking. This is a typical economic approach: consider *all* the costs and benefits, and then compare them. Alternatively, you may not care about any benefits that can be attributed to smoking, because you do not count those benefits as part of social welfare, even if they outweigh the costs of smoking. What you believe should or should not be included in a social welfare analysis is your opinion and is not subject to objective considerations. But if you argue that there are absolutely no benefits to smoking, you are factually incorrect. This is no longer a debate over the accurate measurement of costs and benefits or over the definition of social welfare. You are now, to be polite, unambiguously wrong.

Although few economists are likely to argue that there are no benefits to smoking, there are a growing number of economists who either are not paying much attention to the benefits or simply believe they are not large enough to rule out the role of social policy designed to protect people from themselves. In this chapter, I will consider some of the main arguments in favor of protecting people from themselves, such as misinformed consumers, addiction, advertising, and youth initiation. (The topic of protecting people from *others* will be discussed in the next chapter.) I will use smoking as the main example of indulgent behavior, keeping in mind that other indulgences such as drinking and overeating lend themselves to similar (and often identical) analyses. These other indulgences will also be discussed, but not in a way that simply replicates the smoking analysis.

Throughout this chapter, I want to focus solely on the *paternalistic* aspect of social policy, a topic that has gained much favor among economists lately. While it appears that common sense dictates social control policy to protect others from secondhand smoke, or drunk driving, or escalating health care costs due to rising obesity rates, the sense of protecting people from themselves is far more controversial. What is or isn't common sense, however, when considering *any* justification for social policy from an economic perspective, is never obvious.

WHAT DO YOU KNOW?

Let's return to the basic concept of gains from trade to explain why there must be benefits associated with smoking. If you take out your wallet and pay money for a pack of cigarettes, you absolutely must be benefitting from buying that pack. Any voluntary market transaction necessarily involves gains from trade. Thus, one of the most important benefits of smoking is that of the smoker as a consumer—the benefits as perceived by the smoker must be greater than the price of the pack of cigarettes. When I encounter people who deny the existence of the benefits of smoking, I always ask them to account for why smokers are willing to pay money for something that provides them with no benefits. It's a tough question to answer, but the usual response is that smokers don't understand the risks of what they are doing. That may be true, as there is evidence to suggest that smokers misperceive the true risks of smoking, but it may not be in the way most people think.

The price of a pack of cigarettes is primarily made up of two components—the dollar amount that you have to pay, and a nonmonetary amount that reflects the potential adverse health effects of smoking. When you add the two components together, you have what is known as the *full price* of a pack of cigarettes. The concept of a nonmonetary price can actually include many other components. If you have to travel to purchase a product, or if you devote time and resources to gathering information about the price or quality of a product, these costs make up part of the full price. Your willingness to pay for the product must outweigh the full price in order for you to realize gains from trade from the purchase of that product. For the sake of simplicity, let's assume that the nonmonetary price of a pack of cigarettes just includes the adverse health risk factor.

To use a simple numerical example, assume that the dollar price of a pack of cigarettes is $4 and that each pack imposes a $2 additional health cost on you. If you are a smoker and you correctly understand the risk factor, you will only buy the pack if you value it above the full price of $6. If you value the pack less than $6, you would not get any gains from trade from the purchase. Now let's say you underestimate the risk factor, incorrectly believing it is only $1. If you value the pack above your perceived full price of $5 but less than the true full price of $6, say at $5.50, you will buy the pack, but only because of your misunderstanding of the risk. Had you known the true risk factor, you would not have bought the pack of cigarettes. Thus, underestimating the risk of smoking can lead to too much smoking.

There is also a possibility that you overestimate the risk factor, say at $3. In this case, if you value the pack above the true full price of $6 but less than your perceived full price of $7, say at $6.50, you will not buy the pack, but only because of your misunderstanding of the risk. Had you known the true risk factor, you would have bought the cigarettes. Thus, overestimating the risk of smoking can lead to too little smoking. But what does it mean to smoke *too little*? It means that if you lived in a world with perfect information, you would not constrain your purchase of cigarettes due to your overestimation of the risk factor.

Individuals may underestimate the risk of smoking, or they may overestimate it. What are the social policy implications of these different types of risk misperceptions? If smokers tend to underestimate the risk of smoking, they are likely to be smoking too much relative to the perfect information world. Underestimation of risk represents a classic setting of market failure, and provides a justification for social policy intervention. What policy is best to reduce the amount of smoking is difficult to determine. Should information be provided that can correct the risk misperception? Or should the activity of smoking be more directly controlled through such policies as cigarette taxation or banning?

If smokers tend to overestimate the risk of smoking, the policy implications can be far more subtle. As an economic purist, I could argue that the role of social policy is to provide the correct information to smokers, suggesting that smokers should be made aware that they are smoking too little. Can you imagine the advertising campaign associated with that idea? The overestimation of the risk of smoking implies that there is already a built-in bias that helps reduce the frequency of smoking. This bias, in some sense, acts in the same manner as a tax on cigarettes. Taxes can be used to reduce the consumption of cigarettes. A possible implication of the overestimation of risk, then, is that the tax rate on cigarettes can be reduced. But for some, anything that increases the rate of smoking, even if the increase is optimal in an economic sense, would be ridiculous. Those in favor of completely banning smoking are unlikely to be swayed by the argument that smokers may not be smoking enough.

It is common to see public policies designed to discourage smoking, but policies enacted with the intention of *encouraging* smoking are about as likely to be seen as is Bigfoot at your local shopping mall. Yet if the justification for the policy is lack of perfect information, there may not be much sense to this asymmetric policy stance. If you are misinformed, and the objective is to have you behave *as if* you were perfectly informed, the goal is to determine precisely how you are misinformed. If you underestimate the risk of smoking, the perfectly informed you would smoke less. But if you overestimate the risk of smoking, the perfectly informed you would smoke more. So, is the lack of social policy designed to encourage more smoking due to the fact that people typically underestimate the risk of smoking, or is it because the social goal is not to have you smoke as if you were perfectly informed but instead to simply have you smoke less? To answer this question, I must answer another question: Exactly how do people perceive the risks of smoking?

It is hard to believe that smokers have no understanding at all of the health risks of smoking. The surgeon general's warning on cigarette packages, the antismoking advertising campaigns, and the public condemnation of smoking are all highly visible indicators of the dangers of smoking. But recognizing that there are health risks to smoking does not address the more direct concern of whether smokers overestimate or underestimate the true risks. And keep in mind, smoking doesn't cause bad health outcomes 100 percent of the time—it just increases the probabilities of getting ill or dying. Thus, it certainly is possible that the true risks of smoking are small relative to the perceived risks.

One study provides a nice example of how economists try to measure risk perception using survey data. In a sample of over 3,000 people, each was asked the following question: Among 100 cigarette smokers, how many of them do you think will get lung cancer because they smoke? The *average* answer given was 42.6 percent, while at the time of the study, the best available scientific evidence placed the true lung cancer risk from smoking between 5 percent and 10 percent. Other questions involving the overall mortality risk of smoking (deaths from any smoking-related illnesses), and shortened life expectancy from smoking, yield similar results—people tend to overestimate the risk of smoking. This result is quite broad as it holds for both nonsmokers and smokers, and for young smokers (between the ages of 16 and 21). While it may not be surprising that nonsmokers overestimate the risks of smoking, perhaps partially explaining why they are nonsmokers to begin with, smokers themselves over-estimating the risks suggest that they highly value smoking. Smokers perceive the full price of a pack of cigarettes to be higher than the true full price, yet they still purchase cigarettes.

Then again, there are important caveats to the result that people tend to overestimate the risk of smoking. First, the study finds that *on average* people overestimate the risk. This means that there are many people who also underestimate the risk. Fundamentally, there is a wide heterogeneity in people's risk perceptions, so it is important to stress that the overestimation is just an average result. Second, not all studies find that people overestimate the risk of smoking. One Swed-ish study uses experimental data to determine how much smokers would be willing to pay for a (hypothetically) totally risk-free ciga-rette that is in every way identical to a regular cigarette in terms of appearance and taste but is more expensive. The study found that smokers were not willing to pay very much more for the risk-free cigarettes. This result suggests that smokers likely underestimated the true risk of smoking, because if their risk perceptions were accu-rate, they would have been willing to pay even more for the risk-free cigarettes.

Third, it is possible that people tend to overestimate risks when considering the behavior of others but underestimate risks when considering their own behavior. This is known as *optimism bias*. For example, the survey question above asks to estimate the lung cancer risk of 100 smokers, not to estimate the lung cancer risk *you* face. You may answer 50 percent to the broad question, but when specifically asked about your own lung cancer risk, you may answer 10 percent. Optimism bias does have some empirical support. One study finds that among spouses who both smoke, one spouse's risk perceptions of the health costs of smoking are not affected by the other spouse suffering an adverse health outcome. In other words, even seeing someone very close to you suffer an illness possibly due to smoking does not change the way you perceive your own risks of smoking. Even with optimism bias, it is still important to determine if when you assess your own risk of smoking, you overestimate or underestimate the risks of smoking.

Finally, and some argue most importantly, smoking has the potential to be a lifelong issue. What if it is the case that people, especially teenagers, overestimate the long-term risks of smoking but underestimate the short-term risks? Consider the responses of Oregon high school students to some survey questions about smoking risks. When asked about the long-term risks of smoking, the responses did not differ across three categories of students—nonsmokers, light smokers, and heavy smokers. They all found the long-term risks to be likely. But when asked about the short-term risks, differences appeared. Nonsmokers were most likely to recognize such risks, while heavy smokers were least likely. These results suggest that those students most likely to deny the short-term risks of smoking were most likely to become heavy smokers, starting on a path that could lead to lifetime smoking, even with an expectation of long-term health risks. But as with optimism bias, it is still crucial when discussing risk perceptions to provide some indication of perceived risk relative to true risk. Young smokers may indeed perceive less short-term risk when they are compared to nonsmokers, but that does not directly address the question of whether young smokers underestimate or overestimate the true risk.

Whether smokers truly overestimate the risks of smoking remains an open question. The important point is that risk perceptions may play a key role in justifying social policy to control smoking. But regardless of the risk perceptions of smokers, antismoking advocates usually point to a much more significant factor associated with the costs of smoking—cigarette addiction.

THE ADDICTIVE CHOICE

When you read definitions of the word *addiction*, there's not a lot of pleasant terminology. It is common to see terms like *disease, compulsion, obsession, uncontrollable, harmful, illness*, and so on, in describing addictive behavior. In other words, the definitions tend to be qualitative—addiction is not a good thing. Then economists step into the discussion and change things up with a beautifully simple definition: you are addicted to a product if an increase in your current consumption leads to an increase in your future consumption. This may not be a very exciting definition, but I believe this is one case in which economists have made a substantial contribution—the concept of *rational addiction*.

If you have never heard of the concept of rational addiction, you are probably asking yourself right now: How can anyone put the words *rational* and *addiction* together? Then again, after reading about the concept of *efficient theft* in chapter 3, you are probably getting used to seeing combinations of words that you rarely see together. Rational addiction sounds pretty abstract, but at its core it is really a very intuitive concept. A rational addict's current consumption depends primarily on two things: past consumption and future consumption. The greater the past consumption of an addictive product, the greater will be the current consumption. The greater the anticipated future consumption of an addictive product, also the greater will be the current consumption. In other words, past consumption and future consumption both complement current consumption—the more of one, the more of the other; the less of one, the less of the other.

For example, suppose the government announces that next year, a significant tax increase will be imposed on cigarettes. If you are a smoker, this will make your future smoking more costly for you, and you will smoke less when the time comes. If you are a rational addict, you will incorporate the future cost into your current consumption and consume fewer cigarettes *today*. As another example, suppose there is a temporary stressful event in your life that increases your current consumption of cigarettes. After a few months, you are completely recovered from the stressful event, but you are still consuming more cigarettes than you had been. The increase in your past consumption had a permanent increase in your future consumption. Thus, as a rational addict, you consider your whole time horizon in your decision to smoke.

Often in the literature on addiction, there is a debate about what addiction really means. Is it physical? Is it psychological? Is it a combination of the two? With the economic definition, *any* product or activity can be addictive if an increase in current consumption leads to an increase in future consumption. Cigarettes, alcohol, candy, watching television, shopping on eBay, collecting baseball cards, or exercising can all be addictive. This is a very broad approach, and it does not involve labeling addictive behavior as good or bad.

The main implication of rational addiction theory is that smokers are not entirely overwhelmed or "trapped" by their addiction. As with any product, the demand for cigarettes can be influenced by a number of factors, such as prices, income, advertising, new health information, costs of quitting, and many other things. The thought that an addict must smoke a certain number of cigarettes every day, without the possibility of adjustment based on the factors just listed, does not stand up well to real-world evidence.

Everyone knows someone who is a *former* smoker, suggesting that addicts can change their behavior. Also, there is a substantial body of evidence that shows smokers respond to price changes, such as those caused by tax increases. Ironically, if smokers were trapped by their addiction, the major policy tool used to reduce the burden of addiction—taxation—would not be effective. For tax policy to work, smokers must, at least to some extent, respond rationally to the tax increase and purchase fewer cigarettes. Finally, smokers do seem to take into account the anticipated future costs of their behavior. An often mentioned example of this phenomenon is that when the surgeon general's report about the adverse health effects of smoking was issued in 1964, over the next decade per capita cigarette consumption declined considerably.

While a rational smoker takes into account the costs and benefits of smoking, one prediction of the model is that it is fairly myopic (or impatient) individuals who are most likely to become smokers in the first place. Typically, addicts are thought of as being more impatient than nonaddicts. Addiction is a trade-off between the current benefits the addict reaps from smoking, or drinking, or overeating, and the future cost the addict bears from poorer health or increased heath care costs. Compared to farsighted (or patient) individuals, shortsighted people place little weight on future outcomes, so the current benefits of smoking, for example, are given more weight than the future health costs. Farsighted people, on the other hand, place more weight on future health costs, making them less likely to become smokers today.

It is important to keep in mind, however, that economists typically consider a patience (or impatience) level to be a preference, something that is subjectively determined by each individual. There is no right or wrong patience level, although not everyone agrees with this as many impatient behaviors are considered to be "bad" from a social perspective. Criminals, drug addicts, and especially suicide bombers, are all often thought of as people who place little weight on future outcomes and, therefore, behave badly today. Even smokers are usually thought of as behaving badly, a judgment that does not fit well within the rational addiction model.

From my knowledge of the literature, the concept of rational addiction is accepted much more within the economics profession than outside the profession, which is no surprise. Economists, in general, simply have no problem slapping the word *rational* in front of everything they can think of. But over the past decade or so, there have been some substantial challenges to the rational addiction model from a group of economists who study a field known as *behavioral economics*. Behavioral economists consider what they believe to be are the realistic potential flaws in human behavior. Let's face it, humans are highly complex beings, and even economic models that try to examine the behavior of just a single individual can quickly bog down in unrealistic assumptions and results. In terms of the addiction model, behavioral economists don't abandon the concept of rationality, but they do prod it and twist it and end up with some interesting refinements to the traditional model.

While there have been many such refinements, I will highlight just one to give you an idea of how exposing the economic warts of addictive behavior can quickly expand the complexity of social policy analysis. Let's say you are considering becoming a smoker, and you understand that while there are short-term benefits you will enjoy, there are also long-term health costs you may incur. Here's what you decide to do—you will smoke for three years, then you will quit. That is certainly a simple enough plan. So what will you *actually* do? Let's consider three scenarios.

In the first scenario, you smoke for three years and then you quit. Thus, you actually follow through with your initial plan to quit. This is known as *time consistent* behavior. In the second scenario, you sincerely believe you are going to quit, that is why you start smoking in the first place, but when the three years are up you don't quit. This is known as *time inconsistent* behavior, and it requires some more explanation. Precisely why don't you quit? It is not because the costs or benefits of smoking have changed. Instead, it is the way you *weigh* the costs and benefits that has changed.

When you are time inconsistent, you may be fairly patient in the long term but fairly impatient in the short term. When you consider the costs and benefits of quitting in three years from now, all the costs and benefits are in the future, and so you are fairly patient over the long-term outcomes. You anticipate that your future health three years from now will be important enough to you to make it worth your while to quit. You make the *rational* decision to start smoking today with the intention of quitting. But all future outcomes must one day become current outcomes, and when the three years are up and you are currently making the decision to quit, you are fairly impatient in the short term. Now your future health is not as important to you as you thought it would be, but your short-term gratification from smoking is important to you. *At that time*, your current preference is to continue smoking. You have experienced what is known as a *preference reversal*. Furthermore, you did not anticipate this reversal, so behavioral economists would call you time inconsistent and *naïve*.

Finally, in the third scenario, you plan to smoke for three years then quit, but you recognize that you are time inconsistent and when the time comes you will not quit. Thus, you take action immediately and rationally decide not to start smoking in the first place. Behavioral economists would call you time inconsistent and *sophisticated*. In the end, we are considering three different consumption paths for you: smoke for three years then quit, smoke for three years then don't quit, and don't start to smoke. These three scenarios offer unique behavioral implications.

If you are time inconsistent and naïve, you may come to regret your decision to start smoking in the first place. When the three years are up and you no longer want to quit, you may say to yourself, "I wish I had never started smoking." If you were time consistent instead, you would never experience regret. You make your choice based on future actions that you actually follow through with. So, the feeling of regret is one new, interesting twist behavioral economists have added to the addiction story.

If you are time inconsistent and sophisticated, you anticipate your future preference reversal, so you will not experience regret. Instead, you may practice self-control to prevent yourself from starting to smoke. Remember, your first choice is to smoke for three years then quit, so it may be difficult for you not to start smoking. But by recognizing that you may not quit, you take action to help you not smoke. Maybe you refuse to hang around coworkers or friends who smoke so as not to be tempted. Maybe you use a quitting aid such as a nicotine patch to curb your cravings. If you were time consistent instead, you would not need to practice self-control. So, the practice of self-control is another new twist behavioral economists have added to the addiction story.

In all, the traditional rational addiction model offers an important starting point for how economists approach a controversial issue such as addiction. Behavioral economists have argued, however, that the traditional model does not account for some highly relevant and realistic outcomes, such as addicts experiencing regret over their past behavior or addicts taking (at times extreme) measures to practice self-control. As economists add more complexities to the addiction model, the social policy implications also become more complex, and far more interesting. At the conclusion of this chapter, I will address the justifications for policies designed to protect people from themselves.

COMMERCIAL BREAK

When I was a child, there used to be a wonderful television commercial about a cartoon character named Johnny Smoke. Johnny Smoke was a cartoon cigarette who rode into town on his horse. He wore a black cowboy hat and had on a black mask over his eyes. As Johnny Smoke rode by, cowboys with cigarettes in their mouths starting dropping like flies. Johnny Smoke rode tall in the saddle, and he was the deadliest killer in the West. It was a dark, eerie commercial, and it made a lasting impression on me. Possibly because of Johnny Smoke, I have never taken up smoking. I have also never wanted to be a cowboy.

Johnny Smoke was a clever antismoking commercial. Its purpose was to discourage people from smoking. Whether it was effective is an empirical question, but its goal was clear. Advertising is often criticized for doing exactly what it is designed to do—influence behavior. If advertising leads to behavior that is deemed socially unacceptable, it may be sound social policy to restrict or ban that advertising in an attempt to control the undesirable behavior.

Advertising is a much-criticized activity, especially for such products as tobacco, alcohol, or high-calorie fast foods and snack foods. One specific criticism is that advertising is blamed for making people buy things they do not want or need. From an economic perspective, however, this criticism has little validity. What does it mean to buy something you do not want? If you don't want it, why would you buy it? That may sound simplistic, but it is a very tough question to answer.

The role of advertising is to enhance consumers' value for the product. It may turn a nonpurchaser into a purchaser or a purchaser into a heavier user. Cigarette advertising can bring first-time smokers into the market or increase the amount of smoking by current smokers, but it cannot make people smoke who do not want to smoke. The fact that smokers are willing to pay for cigarettes necessarily implies that they receive gains from trade from smoking. Advertising may simply make some people willing to pay more for cigarettes, thus creating gains from trade that did not previously exist. If the advertising is false or misleading, that is a sound criticism that needs to be addressed. But there are already laws in place that discourage and punish misuse of advertising, although these laws are notoriously difficult and costly to enforce.

Nevertheless, even if advertising in and of itself is not villainous, some may think that certain behaviors that advertising encourages, such as smoking, need to be controlled. Restricting advertising, then, may be an effective policy tool to reduce smoking. But advertising affecting behavior in theory and advertising affecting behavior in practice can be two different things. So an important question must be addressed: Does cigarette advertising actually encourage people to start smoking or smoke more often?

There are numerous empirical studies on the effect of advertising on the demand for cigarettes. Taken as a whole, these studies are extremely inconclusive. Many find little or no effect of advertising on the demand for cigarettes, while others find that there is a demand-enhancing link. Interestingly, those who argue that cigarette advertising does not enhance the demand for cigarettes have the burden of confronting a troubling question: Why do tobacco companies spend hundreds of millions of dollars on advertising?

It may be that studies that show no effect of advertising on cigarette demand all suffer from some of the difficulties in doing empirical work that I identified in chapter 1. Thus, the results of the studies may be unreliable. It may also be that tobacco companies *believe* cigarette advertising enhances demand, even if it really doesn't. Economists, however, generally don't like to think of people or companies making persistent mistakes, especially expensive ones. Or, it may be that cigarette advertising serves a different purpose than enhancing the demand for cigarettes.

Advertising can enhance the demand for cigarettes in two ways: it can increase the *overall* demand for cigarettes in general or it can increase the demand for a specific *brand* of cigarettes. In other words, the Marlboro Man isn't interested in potential new smokers; he only wants to shoot it out with Joe Camel in a duel over existing smokers. Advertising may be used to fight for market share, even if the size of the overall market is stable or declining over time. So when the milk industry uses the slogan "Got Milk?" no brands are mentioned. This type of advertising is designed to bring new milk drinkers into the market or to get current drinkers to drink more. When one specific brand of milk advertises, it may increase the overall demand for milk, or it may simply switch consumers from one brand to another. Economic studies support both views of the effect of advertising on smoking, with many finding an overall effect, and many not finding such an effect.

Ironically, if it is the case that all cigarette advertising is for brand warfare, a total ban on cigarette advertising may be *beneficial* to the tobacco industry. If advertising simply maintains the status quo in market shares, it is ultimately ineffective, and the tobacco companies would save a lot of money by not advertising. But this wouldn't last for long, because each brand would have an incentive to start a big advertising campaign against its rivals while they are not advertising. If advertising is banned, however, the government in effect allows the tobacco industry to eliminate wasteful advertising without worrying about individual brands unilaterally increasing their advertising expenditure.

Some recent studies have taken a different approach to examining the link between advertising and smoking behavior. Instead of seeing if advertising increases the demand for cigarettes, these studies examine if government regulation of advertising reduces the demand. In the United States, for example, in 1971 the government banned cigarette advertising on television and radio. This is known as a *partial* ban, because there are still several other media outlets available for tobacco companies to use, such as newspapers, magazines, outdoor billboards, retail stores, sporting events, and so on. Is it possible that partial bans are not effective in reducing cigarette demand, but *comprehensive* bans would be?

Two separate studies using the same approach look at 22 and 30 countries, respectively, and categorize each country's outlet-banning policy as being weak (advertising banned in two or fewer outlets), limited (banned in three or four outlets), or comprehensive (banned in five or more outlets). The studies found that the greater the number of advertising outlets banned, the lower the per capita cigarette consumption. Thus, advertising bans that are not comprehensive have little impact on smoking, whereas comprehensive bans do have impact. This suggests that there is a link between advertising and smoking when the full media outlet potential is considered. These results hold for a wide range of countries, both developed and developing.

In an environment of substantial antismoking messages, cigarette advertising may be nothing more than an attempt to keep the cigarette market from collapsing too quickly. If this is true, and if the social goal is to reduce cigarette consumption, advertising bans may seem to be an obvious avenue to pursue, but how effective such bans would be is still in question. Furthermore, as I have previously discussed, it is not even clear if reducing cigarette consumption is the appropriate social objective. Certainly, it isn't the only legitimate social objective. While the sense of using social policy to reduce adult smoking is complicated, there is one issue that tends to find a wider consensus: policies designed to reduce *youth* smoking are well founded. It's time to start thinking young.

YOUTHFUL SMOKING

Teenagers have it rough. So many activities that adults take for granted are strictly controlled for teenagers. While the debate over controlling adult smoking is often heated, there tends to be much more agreement (at least among adults) when it comes to controlling teenage smoking. Yet much of the discussion above concerning adult smoking can be applied to teen smoking as well.

There is some evidence that teenagers overestimate the risk of smoking, believing that smoking is more risky than it really is. It is also likely that at least some teenagers are rational in the sense that they take into account the future costs of smoking, although teenagers tend to be more myopic than adults. Furthermore, while cigarette advertising is thought to have a slightly greater effect on teenagers, there is still evidence to suggest that their cigarette consumption may not be significantly influenced by tobacco company advertising expenditure.

There is one more important similarity between teenagers and adults—they both receive gains from trade from purchasing cigarettes. Teenagers are consumers in exactly the same way adults are consumers. A teenager must value a product more than its price to be willing to buy it. Again, we've returned to a consumer sovereignty argument. But this argument has its shortcoming with teenagers. At what age do we believe teenagers have the cognitive ability to make informed decisions about the products they value, especially potentially harmful products? Many may agree that a seventeen- or eighteen-year-old may be old enough to decide what's best to purchase, but hardly anyone would think the same way for a thirteen- or fourteen-year-old.

If you are in favor of banning smoking for everyone, the best way to control teenage smoking is not much of an issue for you. If you believe adults should be allowed to smoke but not teenagers, you are likely to favor a social control policy specifically directed at teenagers. One of the most common of such policies has been to set a minimum age limit for the purchase of tobacco. Although this policy has a commonsense appeal, evidence suggests that the lax enforcement of the age standard at the retail level has greatly undermined its effectiveness in reducing teenage smoking. And while it has been suggested that the policy can be effective if it is rigorously enforced, one must keep in mind that the administration costs of effective enforcement may be huge: there are a lot of cigarette retailers out there. Furthermore, it should also be taken into account that rigorous enforcement of the age standard may just encourage teenagers to become cleverer in finding alternative ways of acquiring cigarettes.

Another policy to deter teenage smoking has to do with restricting the promotional activities of tobacco companies, especially with promotions aimed at the youth market. The Joe Camel advertising campaign has often been criticized precisely for its appeal to teenagers, whether or not that was the explicit intention in the first place. But if it is the case that a teenager's decision to smoke is not significantly influenced by cigarette advertising or other marketing strategies, promotional restrictions may have only a marginal effect on controlling teenage smoking.

The most common social control policy to deter smoking is taxation, but an increased tax rate affects all smokers, not just teenagers. Still, as discussed above, there is evidence to suggest that increased taxation reduces cigarette consumption by at least some amount, and this effect may be larger for teenagers than for adults. But some research has taken a closer look at the differential effects of cigarette taxation on teenagers and adults.

Adults and teenagers who are *current* smokers appear to respond in an identical manner to increased taxation: they consume fewer cigarettes. The key distinction to make is between current smokers (at any age) and those who have *not yet* started to smoke. Once an individual is a smoker, taxation can reduce cigarette consumption. What one study finds, however, is that cigarette taxation has virtually no effect on reducing the *onset* of smoking for teenagers. While this is only a single study, as more empirical studies of this sort are undertaken we may develop a better understanding of the effectiveness of taxation in controlling smoking.

It appears, then, that marketing restrictions, age limits, and taxation may all be limited in how effective they can be in controlling teenage smoking. Interestingly, there are at least two compelling arguments as to why there may be no need to use social policy (and, therefore, social resources) to control teenage smoking. Some argue that there is already a perfect control mechanism in place for teenage smoking that does not involve any social policy intervention— parental control. There is strong evidence to suggest that one of the most effective controls over teenage smoking is the attitude toward smoking in the home. Strict rules against smoking in the home and having parents who do not smoke tend to lead to teenagers who also do not smoke. Actually, it may be easier to justify control policies for adults who do not have the constraint of having to follow their parents' rules than it is to justify such policies for teenagers.

On the other hand, there are those who argue that parents often do not have a strong control over their children, especially outside of the home. Parents may simply be poorly informed about their children's behavior, never realizing that they are smoking or doing other things they are not supposed to be doing. Thus, another justification for social control is that it makes up for lack of parental control. But an even better justification is that the parents themselves may appreciate that they do not have a strong control over their children's behavior and seek assistance from the state in establishing policies to control that behavior.

No doubt, parents may be able to punish their children who behave badly (just ask my parents), but the government may be much better at controlling youth behavior. For example, you may not want your teenager to buy cigarettes or alcohol, but how can you always monitor his or her behavior? The government, however, can make it illegal for retail establishments to sell such product to minors, something parents lack the ability to do. In this sense, parents are like the sophisticated addict discussed earlier. They may recognize that they lack the ability to control their children, so they welcome government controls. The children may not be sophisticated, but the parents may be.

The second compelling argument for why there may be no need to control teenage smoking is more controversial than the first—it may be that young bodies are better able to tolerate indulgences such as smoking, drinking, and overeating, as long as these indulgences taper off over time. In other words, there may simply be no adverse health effects to teenagers who smoke. Of course, a quick rebuttal to this argument is that if you start smoking when you are young, you are likely to continue smoking when you are older and the adverse health effects will kick in. But this is an empirical issue, and one very clever economic study takes advantage of the Vietnam War draft lottery to addresses this concern.

Between 1969 and 1972, some men were randomly considered draft eligible and others were not. The study compares two groups of men (ages 19 and 20)—those who were drafted and served in Vietnam, and those who were not drafted. These groups shared similar characteristics, yet the group that served is predicted to be heavier smokers for several reasons: cigarettes were sold at wholesale prices and tax free on military bases; while in the field, cigarettes were included in the food rations; peer effects were strong, as smoking was common among military men; and military men faced a lot of stress, and high stress levels are associated with increased smoking. Quite simply, the study takes advantage of two groups of men who, in effect, randomly faced different smoking incentives for reasons that were mostly out of their control. This makes for interesting comparisons.

The study offers two key results. The first is that in the short term (5 to 10 years after the lottery), those who served were 35 percent more likely to smoke than those who did not serve. This was an expected result due to the reasons above. The second result is that in the long term (25 to 35 years later), there was no difference in the probability of smoking between the two groups. Furthermore, those who served did not appear to have worse health outcomes later in life compared to those who did not serve. The study offers a strong policy conclusion:

> For health policymakers and consumers in general, our results can be viewed as an affirmation that smoking during young adulthood does not compel one into lifelong smoking, and by quitting in young adulthood one can substantially mitigate longer-term health consequences.

While this conclusion may be a bit strong based on the results of just a single study, it certainly adds a layer of complexity to the issue of youth smoking. Whatever you may think about this study and its policy conclusion based on the result that the young can indulge without much worry about the long-term consequences, when I finish teaching it to my students their eyes light up, and for the rest of the semester attendance is much lower.

If social policy to control teenage smoking is directed specifically at teenagers, the fact that smoking will remain legal for adults will make it that much more difficult for the policy to be effective. Perhaps in the end, maybe the best argument in favor of a comprehensive antismoking policy is that it may be the most effective way to control teenage smoking, and this is a policy objective that many people share. But such a comprehensive policy will have a downside in that it will infringe on the consumer sovereignty of both adults and teenagers, which is a concern of at least some people, even if they are mostly smokers and some economists.

The prevention of teenage smoking may present the strongest justification to control an individual's decision to smoke. But there are many who believe that the absolute strongest (and possibly irrefutable) argument in favor of a social policy to control smoking is to protect others from being harmed by smokers. It is one thing to bear your own risk, but an entirely different thing to impose a risk on others. Protecting people from others will be the topic of the next chapter. For now, let's settle back and enjoy a drink. You may be surprised at the benefits that can bring you.

KEEP DRINKING, IT EVENTUALLY PAYS

In addition to strong public policy concerns over youth smoking, youth (and young adult) alcohol consumption is another important social issue. One serious concern over youth alcohol consumption is how it may affect high school academic performance and advancement. If excessive drinking increases the probability of late graduation or dropping out, students who drink can face long-term adverse consequences. Although there are mixed results, some economic studies confirm these negative consequences. Drinking, especially excessive drinking, has a negative effect on grades. This may be due to increased school absenteeism, or to impairment that reduces concentration during class time, or to drinking taking time away from homework and studying. While lower grades may at first just be a short-term problem, poor academic performance does lead to increased rates of late or no graduation, which in turn both lead to worse job opportunities and lower wages.

For those students who do survive high school and move on to college, drinking may be even more of a concern. Many college students find themselves living away from home for the first time, and this may affect their tendency to engage in risky behaviors. And while most students start college younger than the minimum legal drinking age (MLDA) of 21, most also reach that age during their college years. So even if there are students who abide by the MLDA, it is not long before that constraint is no longer binding.

But there is evidence that a large number of younger college students do not abide by the MLDA. Drinking in college, especially for underage drinkers, appears to have a negative impact on grade point average, to reduce future earnings, and to affect the choice of major (drinkers are more likely to be business majors and less likely to be engineering majors). Yet upper-level students do not fare well in other measures of academic performance. The impact of one more drink, that is, the *marginal* drink, on upper-level students relative to freshmen is that the probabilities of missing a class and falling behind in school both increase.

One culprit in encouraging college drinking is fraternity or sorority membership (for simplicity, in the discussion that follows both fraternity and sorority will be classified with the single term *fraternity*). Approximately 15 percent of American college students join a fraternity, and these students are far more likely to excessively drink in college relative to those not in a fraternity. Perhaps it is the peer pressure that encourages excessive drinking among fraternity members, or the relatively easy access to alcohol through social events, but whatever the case, colleges may be concerned with augmenting whatever social control policies are in place to further curb fraternity influence. One interesting college policy can involve freshman roommate assignment.

One study examines the impact of roommate assignment at Dartmouth College in the early 1990s. Dartmouth assigned roommates based on a handful of criteria, such as gender, smoking, listening to music when studying, neatness, and keeping late hours. Other than those, the assignments were random. The study shows that when one roommate entering college who is likely to join a fraternity is paired with someone who is not likely to join a fraternity, the profraternity roommate tends to influence the other to also join. Thus, the study concludes that college policy that pairs roommates based on the prior expectations to join a fraternity may help reduce college drinking. Two roommates both likely to join a fraternity do not have the ability to influence each other in ways that increase the probability of fraternity membership, and the same holds true for two roommates who are both not likely to join a fraternity.

It is important to note that the inverse relationship between drinking and academic performance may suffer from a reverse causation problem. Is it that drinking adversely affects academic performance, or is it possible that students who perform poorly in school succumb to excessive drinking to alleviate that stress? Are there factors that account for *both* drinking and poor performance? For example, a student who is overly myopic and places little value on future events may be a poor student and an excessive drinker. As for the link between fraternity membership and excessive drinking, that too may involve reverse causation. Perhaps students who have a propensity to drink excessively prior to attending college seek out fraternities to associate with other college students who share similar interests, and even without joining, they will still be heavy drinkers in college.

Whatever the case may be, regardless of the direction of the causation, there is plenty of evidence to suggest that there is an inverse relationship between excessive drinking and academic performance. But there is a light at the end of the tunnel. As an excessive drinker, if you can survive high school and make it into college, and if you can survive college and land yourself a job, your drinking behavior may finally pay off. There is one result that consistently shows up in economic study after economic study—drinkers earn higher wages than nondrinkers. This happy hour result is known as the *drinker's bonus.*

Exactly why does drinking lead to higher wages? Let me start with a confession. I have a drinking problem, and I never realized it until I started reading the research on drinking behavior. It seems that my particular drinking behavior puts me at a greater risk of getting all sorts of illnesses, including high blood pressure, Parkinson's disease, Alzheimer's disease, kidney stones, pancreatic cancer, erectile dysfunction, and a host of others. My drinking problem is that I *don't* drink. Moderate drinking (typically defined as one to three drinks per day) leads to health benefits compared to both excessive drinking *and* abstinence. If I was a moderate drinker, my risks of developing all of the above diseases would decline. Actually, after reading about all that, I take a drink now and then.

So how do the health benefits of moderate drinking tie into higher wages? How much you earn is tied into how productive you are at work. The more productive you are, economists predict, the more you earn. If you are a moderate drinker, relative to someone who abstains, you may be healthier and, therefore, more productive. Furthermore, your better health may lead you to miss fewer days at work, also leading to higher earnings. Excessive drinking typically impairs the worker and leads to more sick days, so this too reduces productivity relative to moderate drinking. In fact, some empirical research shows that moderate drinking does lead to higher wages compared to both abstinence and excessive drinking. However, other research shows that the drinker's bonus holds even for excessive drinking, casting doubt on the productivity explanation.

If it isn't increased productivity that accounts for the drinker's bonus, what other avenue is possible? Drinking is often a social activity, and as such, drinkers have the opportunity to socialize with coworkers, potential clients, employers, and so on. These social connections may improve your earning potential. One interesting study examines this connection by looking at promotions for military officers and enlisted personnel. For enlisted personnel, promotions largely depend on past performance, which is a fairly objective standard to consider.

For officers, however, promotions also depend on future potential, which is more of a subjective concept. Furthermore, enlisted personnel are reviewed by officers who they may not often socialize with, whereas officers may have more social contact with other officers who will consider their promotion. Thus, the social value of drinking is more prominent for officers than for enlisted personnel. Indeed, the study finds that the drinker's bonus exists for both officers and enlisted personnel, but it is far more pronounced for officers.

On the other hand, the drinker's bonus may be explained more simply by considering a different causation. Perhaps more productive workers face more stressful situations while at work and then like to unwind at night with a couple of drinks. In this case, it is productivity increasing drinking, not the other way around. Or perhaps as workers earn higher wages, they purchase more alcohol. In this case, it is higher wages leading to more drinking, not the other way around. Whatever the case may be, there does seem to be a clear *correlation* between drinking and wages, if not a clear *causation*.

From a policy perspective, there is a bit of a paradox for the policy makers to confront. How do they design policies that discourage excessive drinking yet encourage moderate drinking? Increased taxes impact all drinkers. A minimum legal drinking age either allows you to purchase alcohol or not, but it doesn't fine-tune your consumption. Perhaps informing drinkers of the benefits of moderate drinking is the best way to go, but this too may be difficult if the information is not correctly perceived. In all, policy makers may need a drink or two themselves to help them cope with this interesting policy problem.

FAST FOOD (EXPLA)NATION?

One of the most alarming health issues that has developed throughout the last 30 years is the tremendous rise in obesity rates. In 1980, the US adult obesity rate was approximately 15 percent. In 2010 it was close to 34 percent. For children ages 2 to 19, in 1980 the obesity rate was approximately 6 percent, and in 2010 it was 17 percent.

And this isn't only an American phenomenon. Many countries are experiencing similar rises in obesity rates. In the face of these staggering statistics, some economists contribute to the policy debate on controlling obesity with a simple question: Can anyone truly be *overweight*? Is it any wonder why economists aren't often asked to join these debates?

Your weight is determined by basically two things—energy in and energy out. Eating accumulates calories, and physical activity burns them. How much and what type of food you eat, and how much and what type of physical activity you do, largely determines your weight. Aren't all these lifestyle choices nothing more than *choices*? If so, don't we all choose our preferred weight? Of course, our personal choices may be poorly informed, or subject to time inconsistency, or flawed in some other way, but then again, maybe some of us simply prefer to be overweight. However, the concepts of overweight and obese are not defined by individuals but by the medical profession instead.

The most common way to determine if you are overweight or obese is to have your *body mass index* (BMI) calculated. This number is simply calculated by taking your weight (in kilograms) and dividing by your height (in meters) squared. The medical profession classifies weight categories in the following way: for a BMI less than 18.5, you are underweight; for a BMI between 18.5 and 24.9, you are normal weight; for a BMI between 25 and 29.9, you are overweight; and for a BMI above 30, you are obese. (BMI scales are slightly different for children.) From strictly a health perspective, the higher BMIs are associated with many poor health outcomes, and this is why the rapid rise in obesity rates has been a grave concern for health policy officials.

So why have the obesity rates skyrocketed in the past 30 years? Economists, as well as others, have examined many potential explanations, but high up on the list of culprits are fast food restaurants. Not only do they tempt consumers with many quickly served, supersized, high-calorie, and (let's be honest) tasty food options, these restaurants seem to be everywhere: the number of such restaurants more than doubled over the period of rising obesity rates. And with childhood obesity on the rise at alarming rates, fast food restaurants have been facing heightened scrutiny, not only by policy makers but by many health watchdog organizations. There seems to be a public consensus concerning these restaurants—they are increasing the waistlines of their consumers.

Economists have examined several avenues in which fast food restaurants can impact on obesity. One study examines the impact of a local television advertising ban enforced on fast food restaurants and finds large quantitative results—the number of overweight children ages 3 to 11 would be reduced by 18 percent, and for ages 12 to 18, the corresponding reduction would be 14 percent. These numbers may be understated if national and cable television advertising bans can also be enforced, but they may be overstated to the extent that fast food restaurants can increase advertising expenditure in other media outlets. But even if it would be difficult to impose such advertising bans, the study examines an alternative policy approach. If fast food restaurants are prevented from deducting their advertising expenditures from their corporate income tax returns, advertising costs would be higher and fewer ads would be placed. In all, this study finds that fast food advertising does impact on childhood obesity.

In addition to advertising, fast food restaurants often use price promotions to attract new customers or attract customers away from other restaurants. In fact, fast food restaurants devote more marketing resources to price promotions than to advertising. But just as discussed above with cigarette advertising, if one restaurant offers a two-for-one special, will that enhance the demand for fast food from new or existing customers, or will it simply shift customers between brands and not have much impact on eating behavior? One study finds that fast food promotions do increase the quantity of food consumed, as well as switch customers between restaurants. If the policy objective is to discourage fast food consumption, restricting price promotion campaigns may be an effective approach.

One further example of economic research concerning fast food restaurants is a study that examines whether these restaurants being geographically close to schools impacts on student obesity rates. Using a data set that includes the top ten fast food chains and 8,400 public schools in California, the study finds that 7 percent of the schools are located within one-tenth mile of a fast food restaurant, 28 percent within a quarter mile of a restaurant, and 62 percent within a half mile of a restaurant. Factually speaking, then, many schools are close to fast food restaurants. But this doesn't mean that these restaurants *cause* increased obesity rates in school children; that is what the study tries to determine. Looking at ninth graders, the study does find evidence that there is an impact on obesity rates for students in schools within one-tenth mile of a fast food restaurant, but not for schools further away than that.

Although it seems like common sense to believe that fast food restaurants are part of the cause of increased obesity rates, the story is not so simple. These restaurants do not just pop out of thin air—they grow in response to consumer demand. During the period of rapid growth of these restaurants (1972–1997), another phenomenon also occurred. Labor force participation of women also grew, and as more and more families had two working parents, far less time was available to cook meals at home. Fast food restaurants provided a convenient way for time-strapped parents to get dinner for their families. Thus, it is important to examine the precise link between fast food restaurants and obesity. Do these restaurants cause people to become obese, or do people demand these restaurants because of the type of food they serve?

To help sort out this causation issue, one very clever study finds a way to examine the direct link between fast food restaurants and obesity. When new highways are built through rural areas, it is common to see fast food restaurants cluster near the exits. While it is true that local residents may now patronize these restaurants, thus leading to increased obesity rates, the important point is that these restaurants are not being built in response to local consumer demand. They are being built in response to the new highways. This suggests that if there is a relationship between fast food restaurants and obesity, it is the restaurants that are causing the obesity. The study finds that fast food restaurant availability is *not* causing an increase in weight. Thus, while it is easy to blame fast food restaurants for increased obesity rates, other circumstances must be considered.

The economic research on obesity has developed into one of the most active fields in health economics. Economists have studied many other explanations to account for the rise in obesity rates. These explanations have a wide range, including the real price of food falling throughout the twentieth century at the same time the real price of expending calories has risen (less physical labor, more office jobs); the time needed to prepare meals has fallen, leading to more meals (including snacks) per day; cigarette taxes increasing, leading to more eating to compensate for less smoking; snack and soda vending machines located in schools; lax physical education requirements in school (e.g., being able to satisfy the requirement through online courses); cold weather reducing outside activities; and numerous others.

It may not matter what the reason is for increased obesity rates if you attack the issue broadly, such as with taxing fatty foods. Or, it may matter what the reason is if you are trying to fine tune public policy, such as banning vending machines from schools or subsidizing more indoor recreational facilities in cold weather climates. Then again, if weight truly is largely a personal problem for each of us to deal with our BMI demons as we see fit, there may not be any need for social intervention to protect people from themselves at all.

WE WILL MAKE YOU HAPPIER, LIKE IT OR NOT

During all the years I was a student of economics, I don't remember a single lecture in which a professor talked about paternalism as a justification for social policy. Protecting people from themselves just doesn't make much sense when talking about rational economic behavior. At most, traditional economic reasoning would consider a lack of perfect information as a rationale for social intervention, but the typical policy fix would be to provide the correct information and then let people decide for themselves what best to do.

While paternalism used to be a four-letter word to most economists, that has been changing over the past decade or so, as more and more economists are identifying scenarios in which paternalistic policies can be justified. I am going to analyze one such scenario, already introduced earlier in this chapter. Assume you are considering becoming a smoker. You are fully informed of *all* the costs and benefits of smoking, and you decide it is in your best interest to start smoking now and then quit in three years. You may be time consistent or time inconsistent, and if the latter, you may be sophisticated or naïve. How well does paternalism as a justification for policy intervention hold up in each case?

If you are time consistent, there is little (or no) justification for controlling your behavior. Any consumption path you choose, you will stick with. You will never want to practice self-control, and you will never regret any decision you make. Controlling your behavior can only make you worse off. However, if you are time inconsistent and sophisticated, this may present a strong justification for social policy to control your behavior, but only under one condition—you welcome the control.

By being sophisticated, you recognize your potential for time inconsistent behavior. You know if you start smoking today with the intention of quitting in three years, when the time comes you may choose not to quit. In anticipation of this preference reversal, you may want to practice self-control, but that may not be easy for you to do, so you welcome social policy to help you control your behavior. In fact, there is some empirical evidence to support this premise.

One study finds that increased cigarette taxation makes *smokers* happier. This is an unusual result when considering the standard economic model of consumption in which taxes make people worse off. How happy would you be if on your next trip to the grocery store all your purchases cost you 10 percent more? Yet the study finds that by using US data that include happiness measures, smokers, on average, appreciate cigarette taxes. This result is also confirmed using similar data from Canada. Furthermore, the study examines the effect of other taxes (such as beer or gas taxes) and finds that these taxes do not make smokers happier, suggesting that these people don't just enjoy being taxed (a comforting result to an economist). If cigarette taxes are making some smokers happier, it may be because these smokers are time inconsistent and sophisticated.

Another common antismoking policy control is to ban smoking in certain public places. These bans are not only supported by nonsmokers, but they are also supported by current smokers. For example, using survey data from 2001 to 2002, 69.4 percent of people classified as never smokers favored smoking bans in indoor work areas, and 51 percent of smokers also favored such bans. The degree of those favoring bans, however, depends on the specific venues being considered. For bars and cocktail lounges, 43 percent of never smokers and 8.9 percent of smokers favor bans. For hospitals, 91.4 percent of never smokers and 74.2 percent of smokers favor bans. But just because many smokers favor bans, that does not directly tell us *why* they favor them.

Smokers may favor bans to help with their lack of self-control, consistent with the above reasoning for why cigarette taxes make smokers happier. On the other hand, smokers may favor bans to protect others from their own secondhand smoke, or to protect their family and friends from the secondhand smoke of other smokers. To help sort out these conflicting reasons, one clever study partitions the smokers into three groups: those who tried to quit and plan to try again, those who plan to try to quit for the first time, and those who do not plan to quit. If smokers favor bans as a self-control mechanism, it is likely that those who have quit in the past or who plan to quit may be more likely to favor bans than those who never plan to quit. Indeed, the results of the survey show that for restaurant bans, for example, 24.4 percent of those who have tried to quit, 21.4 percent of those who want to try, and only 12.4 percent of those with no plans to quit favor bans. This same ranking holds true for other venues. This provides some evidence that people who recognize that they have been unsuccessful quitters may welcome social policy to help them reduce their opportunities to smoke.

It should be noted that just because sophisticated time inconsistent smokers may welcome social policy to help them with their lack of self-control, this does not suggest that they always favor specific government interventions. Perhaps a smoker with self-control problems appreciates workplace smoking bans but does not appreciate increased cigarette taxes. Still, to the extent that smokers demand control policies from their policy officials, this is a strong justification for policy intervention.

Finally, what about the justifications for protecting naïve time inconsistent smokers from themselves? At first blush, there seems to be strong justifications for protecting the naïve. You plan on starting to smoke with the explicit intention of quitting in three years, but when the time comes, you do not quit. It was *your* intention to quit in the first place, so controlling your behavior is, in a sense, what you prefer. This sounds a lot like the sophisticated smoker we just discussed, but there is an important difference. If you are sophisticated, you know you won't quit in three years. If you are naïve, you don't appreciate that you have a self-control problem. So in this case, can we design social policy that makes you better off even if you don't welcome the intervention? The short answer is no.

The common way to control smoking is through taxation or restricting your ability to smoke in certain venues. Do these policies make you better off? Not at all. Because you believe you will quit in three years, you don't appreciate any controls that make it more expensive or difficult for you to smoke. What if a policy can be specifically designed that will let you smoke for three years and then makes you quit? This matches your initial intentions, so will this policy make you better off? Once again, not at all. While quitting is what you wanted to do, after three years it is no longer what you want to do. A preference reversal may be regretful, but it is still a *preference*. If left to your own devices, no one is forcing you not to quit in three years. You *choose* not to quit.

The behavioral economists who consider naïve behavior have developed a paternalistic catch-22—if you truly are naïve, you may act in ways against your own best interests, but your naïvety also prevents you from appreciating any measures that try to protect you from yourself. It can get even worse. In some economic models of naïvety, the individual is naïve about being naïve. You would think that once the three years pass and you don't quit, you now know about your time inconsistent behavior and so you become sophisticated. But that may not be the case if you simply reset your thinking and tell yourself you will smoke for three more years *then* quit. For example, how many of us have started a month-long diet *every* Monday of the month? If the goal of paternalistic social policy is to make naïve people better off, it fails, miserably. Unless somewhere along the way the naïve person explicitly says, "Thank you for controlling my indulgent behavior," the paternalistic policy cannot make that person better off *in his or her own mind.*

Where does this leave us? If we can't make the naïve better off with policies designed to protect them from themselves, we need to reconsider the social objective. Instead of making the naïve better off, the goal can be to improve social welfare. But this is tricky. Consider a society made up entirely of naïve time inconsistent smokers. We restrict their smoking behavior. If each member of our society does not appreciate the intervention, how can we argue that social welfare has improved? Instead of talking about the preferences of the people we are trying to protect, we consider what are known as *ideal* preferences.

Ideal preferences hold people to behavior that is defined outside of their true preferences. If we define not smoking as the ideal, social welfare is improved if we encourage people not to smoke, regardless of how they feel about the policies. The obvious problem here is to define "ideal" behavior. Sometimes the naïve smoker may help us with this task. You plan on quitting in three years, so you yourself identify the ideal. Even if you have a preference reversal, the ideal was generated by your own initial preferences. But this won't be possible in most settings. The ideal will have to be defined by policy officials, and this allows the policy intervention door to be opened wide, very wide. And this is why I think many economists are now taking the peculiar step of promoting good health. Why is this peculiar?

Economists interested in social policy have traditionally focused on broad objectives, such as enhancing well-being, when considering policy interventions. Good health is a much narrower concept than well-being. By promoting good health, indulgences such as smoking, drinking, and overeating can be considered as unhealthy, immediately justifying policies to reduce these indulgences. But if you consider well-being instead, which allows for people to experience enjoyment from these activities, the immediate debate is over whether there is any sense to paternalistic policies in the first place. The answer may be yes, and then a discussion of which policies to enact becomes relevant. However, the answer may be no, as the benefits of these indulgences may well exceed the costs.

Paternalism is always going to be tough sell to many people. The key point I am trying to make is not that it is difficult to justify paternalistic policies. Quite the opposite. The notion of ideal preferences is well understood in economic analysis, and the concept of social welfare has always been, and always will be, subjectively determined. But if the justification is that you are making people better off, that may simply not be the case. Paternalistic social policy needs to be considered carefully. Then again, perhaps it need not be considered at all. Policies designed to reduce indulgent behavior can be justified far more traditionally by arguing that the policies are designed to protect people from *others*. We turn to this argument in the next chapter.

NOTES

The quotation about the lack of concrete benefits of smoking can be found in an exchange of three letters to the editor in *Regulation* 18, no. 4 (1995): 5–7.

The survey article "The Economics of Smoking" is written by Frank J. Chalouopka and Kenneth E. Warner, and can be found in *Handbook of Health Economics*, ed. Anthony J. Culyer and Joseph P. Newhouse (Amsterdam: Elsevier, 2000), 1541–1627.

Evidence on smokers' risk perceptions is presented in W. Kip Viscusi, *Smoke-Filled Rooms* (Chicago: University of Chicago Press, 2002), chapter 7. Also see his article "Do Smokers Underestimate Risk?" *Journal of Political Economy* 98 (1990): 1253–69. For an interesting exchange about smokers' risk perceptions, see the papers in the *Journal of Behavioral Decision Making* 13 (2000): W. Kip Viscusi, "Comment: The Perils of Qualitative Smoking

Risk Measure," 267–71; Paul Slovic, "What Does It Mean to Know a Cumulative Risk? Adolescent Perceptions of Short-Term and Long-Term Consequences of Smoking," 259–66; and Paul Slovic, "Rejoinder: The Perils of Viscusi's Analysis of Smoking Risk Perceptions," 273–76.

Two other papers on risk perceptions are by Henrik Hammar and Olof Johansson-Stenman, "The Value of Risk-Free Cigarettes: Do Smokers Underestimate the Risk?" *Health Economics* 13 (2004): 59–71; and Ahmed Khwaja, Frank Sloan, and Sukyung Chung, "Learning about Individual Risk and the Decision to Smoke," *International Journal of Industrial Organization* 24 (2006): 683–99.

The seminal article on rational addiction is by Gary S. Becker and Kevin M. Murphy, "A Theory of Rational Addiction," *Journal of Political Economy* 96 (1988): 675–700. For an updated discussion, see Jonathan Gruber and Botond Koszegi, "Is Addiction Rational? Theory and Evidence," *Quarterly Journal of Economics* 116 (2001): 1261–1303.

Addiction and time inconsistency is thoroughly developed in the research of Ted O'Donoghue and Matthew Rabin. For two examples of their work, see "Addiction and Self-Control," in *Addiction: Entries and Exits*, ed. J. Elster (New York, NY: Russell Sage Foundation Press, 1999); and "Self Awareness and Self Control," in *Now or Later: Economic and Psychological Perspective on Intertemporal Choice*, ed. R. Baumeister, G. Loewenstein, and D. Read (New York, NY: Russell Sage Foundation Press, 2001).

For an interesting and accessible debate on smoking with emphasis on time inconsistency, see the series of articles in *Regulation* 25, no. 4 (2003): 52–72. The articles are by Jonathan Gruber, "Smoking's Internalities"; W. Kip Viscusi, "The New Cigarette Paternalism"; Thomas A. Firey, "My Future Self and I"; and Gio Batta Gori, "Less Hazardous Smokes?"

The very best thing about the Internet is that you can now watch the Johnny Smoke commercial on YouTube.

For two overviews of the impact of advertising and the demand for cigarettes, see Jon P. Nelson, "Cigarette Advertising Regulation: A Meta-Analysis," *International Review of Law and Economics* 26 (2006): 195–226; and Rajeev K. Goel, "Cigarette Advertising and U.S. Cigarette Demand: A Policy Assessment," *Journal of Policy Modeling* 31 (2009): 351–57.

The two studies of comprehensive tobacco advertising bans are by Henry Saffer and Frank Chaloupka, "The Effect of Tobacco Advertising Bans on Tobacco Consumption," *Journal of Health Economics* 19 (2000): 1117–37; and Evan Blecher, "The Impact of Tobacco Advertising Bans on Consumption in Developing Countries," *Journal of Health Economics* 27 (2008): 930–42.

The study of cigarette taxes and the onset of teenage smoking is by Philip DeCicca, Donald Kenkel, and Alan Mathios, "Putting Out the Fires: Will Higher Taxes Reduce the Onset of Youth Smoking?" *Journal of Political Economy* 110 (2002): 144–69.

For papers on various aspects of youth smoking behavior, see Lisa M. Powell and Frank Chaloupka, "Parents, Public Policy, and Youth Smoking," *Journal of Policy Analysis and Management* 24 (2005): 93–112; and Lisa M. Powell, John A. Tauras, and Hana Ross, "The Importance of Peer Effects, Cigarette Prices and Tobacco Control Policies for Youth Smoking Behavior," *Journal of Health Economics* 24 (2005): 950–68.

The Vietnam draft and smoking behavior paper is by Daniel Eisenberg and Brian Rowe, "The Effect of Smoking in Young Adulthood on Smoking Later in Life: Evidence Based on the Vietnam Era Draft Lottery," *Forum for Health Economics and Policy* 12 (2009): 1–32.

Two papers on drinking and high school academic performance by Francesco Renna are "The Economic Cost of Teen Drinking: Late Graduation and Lowered Earnings," *Health Economics* 16 (2007): 407–19; and "Teens' Alcohol Consumption and Schooling," *Economics of Education Review* 27 (2008): 69–78.

Two papers on drinking and college academic performance are by Amy M. Wolaver, "Effects of Heavy Drinking in College on Study Effort, Grade Point Average, and Major Choice," *Contemporary Economic Policy* 20 (2002): 415–28; and Lisa M. Powell, Jenny Williams, and Henry Wechsler, "Study Habits and the Level of Alcohol Use among College Students," *Education Economics* 12 (2004): 135–49.

Two papers on drinking and fraternities by Jeff DeSimone are "Fraternity Membership and Binge Drinking," *Journal of Health Economics* 26 (2007): 950–67; and "Fraternity Membership and Drinking Behavior," *Economic Inquiry* 47 (2009): 337–50. The Dartmouth college roommate study is by Bruce Sacerdote, "Peer Effects with Random Assignment: Results for Dartmouth Roommates," *Quarterly Journal of Economics* 116 (2001): 681–704.

Papers on the drinker's bonus are by Gary A. Zarkin et al, "Alcohol Use and Wages: New Results from the National Household Survey on Drug Abuse," *Journal of Health Economics* 17 (1998): 53–68; Jeremy W. Bray, "Alcohol Use, Human Capital, and Wages," *Journal of Labor Economics* 23 (2005): 279–312; Philip J. Cook and Bethany L. Peters, "The Myth of the Drinker's Bonus," NBER Working Paper No. 11902 (2005); and Bethany L. Peters, "The Drinkers' Bonus in the Military: Officers versus Enlisted Personnel," *Applied Economics* 41 (2009): 2211–20.

Papers on obesity and fast food restaurants are by Shin-Yi Chou, Michael Grossman, and Henry Saffer, "An Economic Analysis of Adult Obesity: Results from the Behavioral Risk

Factor Surveillance System," *Journal of Health Economics* 23 (2004): 565–87; Inas Rashad and Michael Grossman, "The Super Size of America: An Economic Estimation of Body Mass Index and Obesity in Adults," *Eastern Economic Journal* 32 (2006): 133–48; Shin-Yi Chou, Inas Rashad, and Michael Grossman, "Fast-Food Restaurant Advertising on Television and Its Influence on Childhood Obesity," *Journal of Law and Economics* 51 (2008): 599–618; Timothy J. Richards and Luis Padilla, "Promotion and Fast Food Demand," *American Journal of Agricultural Economics* 91 (2009): 168–83; Janet Currie et al, "The Effect of Fast Food Restaurants on Obesity," *American Economic Journal: Economic Policy* 2 (2010): 32–63; and Michael L. Anderson and David A. Matsa, "Are Restaurants Really Supersizing America?" *American Economic Journal: Applied Microeconomics* 3 (2011): 152—88.

Other interesting papers on the economics of obesity are by Tomas J. Philipson and Richard A. Posner, "Is the Obesity Epidemic a Public Health Problem? A Review of Zoltan J. Acs and Alan Lyles's *Obesity, Business, and Public Policy*," *Journal of Economic Literature* 46 (2008): 974–82; and David M. Cutler, Edward L. Glaeser, and Jesse M. Shapiro, "Why Have Americans Become More Obese?" *Journal of Economic Perspectives* 17 (2003): 93–118.

The article on cigarette taxes making smokers happier is by Jonathan H. Gruber and Sendhil Mullainathan, "Do Cigarette Taxes Make Smokers Happier?" *Advances in Economic Analysis and Policy* 5 (2005): 1–43. The article on smokers supporting smoking bans is by Joni Hersch, "Smoking Restrictions as a Self-Control Mechanism," *Journal of Risk and Uncertainty* 31 (2005): 5–21.

There are many scholarly articles debating the role of paternalistic social policy. For a small sampling of this literature, see the papers by Wolfgang Pesendorfer, "Behavioral Economics Comes of Age: A Review Essay on *Advances in Behavioral Economics*," *Journal of Economic Literature* 44 (2006): 712–721; George Loewenstein and Ted O'Donoghue, "'We Can Do This the Easy Way or the Hard Way': Negative Emotions, Self-Regulation, and the Law," *University of Chicago Law Review* 73 (2006): 183–206; Christine Jolls and Cass R. Sunstein, "Debiasing through Law," *Journal of Legal Studies* 35 (2006): 199–241; Edward L. Glaeser, "Paternalism and Psychology," *University of Chicago Law Review* 73 (2006): 133–56; Drew Fudenberg, "Advancing beyond *Advances in Behavioral Economics*," *Journal of Economic Literature* 44 (2006): 694–711; and Richard H. Thaler and Cass R. Sunstein, "Libertarian Paternalism," *AEA Papers and Proceedings* 93 (2003): 175–79.

This chapter was based on a tremendous amount of reading I did to write the book *The Economics of Excess: Addiction, Indulgence, and Social Policy* (Stanford, CA: Stanford University Press, 2011). See that book for a fuller discussion of the topics introduced in this chapter and a much more extensive list of references.

6 *Stop Bothering Me*

A FACTORY'S PRODUCTION process emits smoke pollution into the air. An oil tanker transports oil and, due to an accident, spills oil into the ocean and along the coast. Airports have takeoff and landing patterns that disturb neighboring residents. Secondhand smoke causes cancer in nonsmokers. People talk in movie theaters. Your roommate's television is too loud. Students walk into the classroom late. This opening paragraph is starting to annoy you. Each of these situations provides an example of what economists refer to as a *negative externality*. Or more simply put: people hate to be bothered.

A negative externality is when an individual's private action imposes a cost on another individual. For example, the owner of a factory may only be concerned with selfishly maximizing profit and not with the consequences of the pollution emitted into the air. Thus, private actions may impose *social* costs, and laws and regulations are often designed to control these costs. But the concept of a negative externality can be extremely broad, and what type of externalities deserve the attention of social regulators can be an intriguing question.

I often present my students with the following two scenarios and ask them whether, from a social policy perspective, the two differ. In the first scenario, it is two in the morning and your neighbors are having a loud party and the noise is keeping you from getting any sleep. In the second scenario, it is two in the morning and your neighbors are having a quiet party that is keeping you from getting any sleep because you are upset that you weren't invited. In both scenarios, your neighbors are imposing a negative externality upon you by keeping you from sleeping. Do you believe there is a difference between the two settings?

When I pose that question to my students, they usually claim that there is a difference. In the first case, you are being physically bothered by an identifiable noise. If the party is loud, anyone can observe there is a possibility of an externality. It may be extremely difficult to determine the extent of the externality (in terms of a dollar equivalent), but designing a social policy to stop loud parties is certainly feasible. In the second case, the externality is not easily observed by others. Your hurt feelings can only be verified by you, and this provides a very difficult justification for social intervention. But from a theoretical perspective, I contend that there is little difference between the two settings. The externality of the ongoing party is that you can't sleep. One is a *physical* externality, that is, the loud noise keeps you awake. The other is a *psychic* externality, that is, your hurt feelings keep you awake. The key point, however, is that in both cases you are being hurt.

For the most part, legal cases in which damages may be assessed deal with physical externalities. This makes good sense because physical damages are more likely to be measurable than are psychic damages. But psychic externalities motivate a lot of social policy. In chapter 3, I discussed different policies to increase the supply of organs for transplant that are usually dismissed for being repugnant. Many people against these policies would not be physically harmed by their adoption, yet they are still deemed offensive. Other examples include so-called victimless crimes, such as drug use, gambling, and prostitution, that are often decried by individuals who are never physically affected by any of these activities. This chapter is devoted to physical externalities and will eventually focus on the issue of secondhand smoke. But I think it is worth keeping in mind that social policy can be motivated by many factors.

THERE GOES THE SUN

Can anyone own the sun? This seemingly ridiculous question has, in some sense, been at the heart of several lawsuits, including the following two. In a 1959 case, two neighboring luxury hotels in Florida went to court to settle a property dispute. The Fountainebleau Hotel began constructing a fourteen-story addition that, when completed, would cast a shadow in the afternoon over the swimming pool and sunbathing area of the Eden Roc Hotel. The Eden Roc Hotel wanted the right to prevent the additional construction, claiming that the blocking of the sunlight adversely affected its business by reducing its guests' enjoyment. In a 1982 case, the owner of a solar-heated house, Prah, sued the owner of a neighboring property, Maretti, who was building a house. Maretti's house, when completed, would block the sunlight from reaching Prah's solar panels and prevent the solar heating system from being effective. In both cases, the ultimate question to be addressed is this: Does one party have the right to block the sunlight from reaching the other party?

When I ask my students to resolve these cases, the general feeling they convey is that the Fountainebleau Hotel should have the right to build the addition, but Maretti should not have the right to build his house. The reasoning offered is that blocking the sunlight from reaching a swimming pool and sunbathing area is not that important, but blocking sunlight from reaching a solar-heated house is important. At this point in the lecture, I have to congratulate my students. With no knowledge of how the real-world cases were decided, my students exactly matched the reasoning used by the courts in settling the real disputes.

In the Prah case, the court argued that

Access to sunlight has taken on a new significance in recent years. In this case the plaintiff seeks to protect access to sunlight, not for aesthetic reasons or as a source of illumination but as a source of energy. Access to sunlight as an energy source is of significance both to the landowner who invests in solar collectors and to a society which has an interest in developing alternative sources of energy.

This reasoning, in part, led to Prah winning his case. The earlier case, however, was lost by the Eden Roc Hotel. Do you agree with my students and the courts and believe these were the right decisions? I do, but only because I don't think it mattered at all how the courts decided either of these cases. But before I explain that, I'd like to examine the court's reasoning behind the Prah decision.

At first blush, it sounds correct that sunlight is more important for energy purposes than it is for aesthetic purposes. Does it really matter that the Eden Roc's guests will have less sunlight for swimming and tanning purposes? The answer is yes, it does matter. If part of the attraction of staying at the Eden Roc is the location of the pool and sunbathing area, lack of sunlight will diminish the Eden Roc's value to its guests. This loss in value could translate into substantial lost profit to the Eden Roc. In other words, the Eden Roc values the sunlight hitting the pool area, and if the sunlight is blocked, the Fountainebleau is imposing a negative externality on the Eden Roc. The court in the Prah case may not value sunlight for aesthetic purposes, but it is not the court that is incurring the externality. One can just as easily argue that there is little value to solar energy given that there are alternative heat sources that Prah can use.

More substantially, the court in the Prah case is making the wrong comparison. It doesn't matter at all how the value of the sunlight to a homeowner compares to the value of the sunlight for a hotel. The homeowner and the hotel do not have conflicting interests. The key comparison in each case is the value of sunlight to one party versus the value of blocking the sunlight to the other party. If we consider the goal of allocating resources to their highest-valued use, determining the highest-valued use is at issue in each case. Fortunately, that determination may never have to be explicitly made.

Let's make up some hypothetical numbers for ease of explanation. Assume that the Eden Roc values the sunlight at $1 million, and the Fountainebleau values the extension that blocks the sunlight at

$2 million. Furthermore, assume that the court has no idea what either of these values are. How should the court decide? It doesn't matter. Regardless of its decision, the extension will be built. If the court rules in favor of the Eden Roc, the Fountainebleau will be willing to pay up to $2 million to build the extension. Because the Eden Roc only needs a minimum of $1 million, there are *gains from trade* that can make both hotels better off if the extension is built. Exactly how the gains from trade are shared depends upon the relative bargaining strengths of the two hotels. But it is in both of their best interests to have the extension built. What if the court rules against the Eden Roc? The exact same result will occur. The Fountainebleau Hotel will build its extension unless the Eden Roc can pay it at least $2 million not to build. But with the Eden Roc's value at only $1 million, there are no gains from trade to prevent the extension from being built. In either case, the highest-valued use ends up being realized.

If we were to switch the numbers around, giving the Eden Roc the higher-valued use of $2 million and the Fountainebleau the lower-valued use of $1 million, it still wouldn't matter what the court decides. The gains from trade would lead to the extension not being built, which is now the higher-valued use. If the court rules in favor of the Eden Roc, the Fountainebleau would not be willing to pay $2 million to build its extension. If the court rules in favor of the Fountainebleau, the Eden Roc would be willing to pay at least $1 million (and at most $2 million) to keep the extension from being built. All the court has to do is give one of the two parties the property right over the sunlight. After that, the parties can negotiate their way to the efficient outcome.

An identical analysis can be used for the Prah case. Whoever has the highest-valued use will end up having his way, whether he is awarded the property right or he has to pay the other party. Both of these cases are similar to the Moore case (from chapter 3) involving the doctor who profited from taking his patient's cells. In that case, I argued that the gains from trade were so phenomenal that it wouldn't matter what the court did—the cells would eventually end up in the hands of the doctor. Either the doctor would have the right to take the cells without paying compensation or the patient would have the right to sell his cells. But even when it isn't obvious who has the highest-valued use, as in the sunlight cases, as long as the property right is well defined, the highest-valued use will be achieved.

Throughout all of these analyses, though, I am assuming that the parties will actually negotiate to resolve their dispute once the property right is assigned. In the Moore case, this is almost guaranteed given that there were hundreds of millions of dollars to be shared. But what about more modest cases, like Fountainebleau or Prah, where the gains from trade may be anywhere from hundreds of thousands of dollars to just thousands of dollars? If, for whatever reasons, the negotiation costs are high, the parties may not be able to exploit the gains from trade. What can the courts do in these cases?

THERE'S NO TALKING TO SOME PEOPLE

When two parties refuse to negotiate with each other, the highest-valued use may not be achieved. The fact that the two parties are in court seems to suggest that they are not working out their problems in the first place. But there are two separate issues here. In the hotel case, the two hotels were not working out their problem because there was a lack of a *well-defined property right*. The Eden Roc didn't actually have the right to unrestricted sunlight, just as the Fountainebleau didn't actually have the right to block the sunlight. If neither party can recognize that one of them does have the well-defined right to some action, how can negotiation take place? So, the first issue is to establish a well-defined property right, which means that the court can make it clear which party has the right over the sunlight. In the hotel case, the Fountainebleau was given the right to build the extension. In the solar energy case, Prah was given the right to stop Maretti from blocking the sunlight.

Once a property right is established, the second issue the court must deal with is how that right should be protected. One simple way to protect a property right is to use a *property rule*. What this entails is, in effect, absolutely nothing. A property rule indicates that the court will not offer any further intervention after the property right is assigned. With a well-defined right, the parties are left to their own devices to work out whatever problems they may have. Once the Fountainebleau is given the right to build the extension, the only way to prevent it from doing so is for the Eden Roc to negotiate an agreement not to have the extension built. This will only occur if the Eden Roc values the sunlight more than the Fountainebleau values the extension *and* if the two parties are willing to negotiate.

When negotiation costs are high, and parties are unlikely to negotiate, a property rule may not achieve the efficient outcome. Unless the court knows the highest-valued use and assigns the property right to that party, there is no guarantee that the highest-valued use will be achieved. If the court assigns the right to the lower-valued use and no further negotiation will take place, an inefficient outcome will result. Thus, a property rule coupled with high negotiation costs may not be efficient.

Another way to protect a property right is to use a *liability rule*. After assigning a property right, the court can set a damage payment schedule that can allow one party to affect the actions of another party. For example, assume in the hotel case that the court knows the Fountainebleau values the extension at $2 million but does not know what the value of the sunlight is to the Eden Roc. Thus, the court does not know what the highest-valued use is. Unless the court luckily assigns the property right to the highest-valued use, using a property rule in this case may not lead to the efficient outcome if the parties won't negotiate. Instead, the court can use the limited information it has to achieve the efficient outcome. The court knows what the Fountainebleau's value is, so it should assign the property right to the Fountainebleau. But now, it can allow the Eden Roc to prevent the building of the extension only if it pays the Fountainebleau $2 million. A liability rule that dictates the payment schedule allows for one party to influence the behavior of another party without any negotiation. If the Eden Roc values the sunlight at more than $2 million, it will be worth paying the $2 million to keep the extension from being built, and that would be the highest-valued use. If the Eden

Roc values the sunlight at less than $2 million, it will not pay and the extension will not be built, and now that would be the highest-valued use.

Although the sunlight examples are fairly simplistic, you can apply the above economic reasoning to any negative externality setting, such as those presented in the opening paragraph of this chapter. To the extent that individuals can negotiate, the assignment of the property right is the key aspect of resolving a negative externality. If the parties can't (or won't) negotiate, a property rule can only work if the efficient outcome is known. If the efficient outcome is not known but some information is available, a liability rule may allow for the efficient outcome to be achieved. If no information at all is available, it is very difficult to efficiently resolve a negative externality the parties can't resolve themselves.

Of course, what is meant by the efficient outcome will depend on the definition of social welfare. For example, in the case of secondhand smoke, the efficient outcome may involve some trade-off between the benefits smokers receive and the costs they impose on nonsmokers. Or, if you are an antismoking advocate, you may support a complete ban on smoking in public places, because you don't count the benefits smokers receive as part of the social welfare. The issue of secondhand smoke provides more than just an abstract example, however, as it is one of the most contentious negative externality issues currently facing society.

SMOKE GETS IN YOUR EYES AND NOSE AND THROAT

One day I was sitting in a restaurant with my father, and for some reason we started talking about smoking in public. My father is a rabid antismoker, and he believes there are absolutely no benefits to smoking. This is understandable as he has seen several of his friends who were lifelong smokers become ill or die. Needless to say, he was arguing strongly in favor of banning smoking in public places. Just for fun, I decided to take the opposite position. When I returned home after the meal, I told my mother about the conversation I had with my father, expecting her to side with me. To my great surprise, my mother agreed with my father. After over fifty-five years of marriage, I guess it was bound to happen at least once. Although my father was unyielding to my arguments, I decided to use one of my favorite arguing techniques with my mother—the hypothetical situation.

Let's say my mother is hosting a bridge party at her home, and she invites several friends to attend. Some of her friends happen to be smokers, and others are nonsmokers. What are the possible scenarios? My mother can decide that no smoking is allowed in her home. Her smoking friends can either not smoke or go outside to smoke. Alternatively, they can simply not play bridge. Now let's say my mother decides that it is okay for anyone to smoke in her home. Her nonsmoking friends can put up with the smoke, not play bridge, or ask the smokers to refrain from smoking. Either everyone will come to some mutually agreeable solution or there will be no bridge game. I asked my mother the following question: "Would you want the government to tell you that if you are going to invite people into your home, you must have a nonsmoking home?" She immediately replied, "Of course not!" Then I asked her how she would feel if she owned a restaurant and the government told her she couldn't allow her customers to smoke. I think she appreciated the point I was making. Actually, I think she just needed any excuse to once again disagree with my father.

In the smoking/antismoking war, a key debate is over the banning of smoking in public places. Many nonsmokers may not care if smokers want to make the private decision to smoke, but when it comes to secondhand smoke (also called environmental tobacco smoke, or ETS) there is no such acceptance. Although there is a substantial scientific debate about the health effects of ETS (which I will discuss later in this chapter), for now I'm going to assume that secondhand smoke does create adverse health effects in nonsmokers. But just as with most pollution examples, it is not difficult to accept that one person's actions can impose costs on another person. The difficult question involves the appropriate trade-off between the polluter and the victim.

Unlike the examples involving the two hotels or the two neighbors, it is extremely unlikely that smokers and nonsmokers will generally be able to negotiate a solution. Negotiations may be possible in situations like the bridge party example, or with roommates, but in settings involving strangers gathering in a restaurant or bar, there appears to be little room for market solutions to be effective. This may help explain why there is a loud outcry against smoking in public places, and why many localities have banned smoking in bars and restaurants. But despite the fact that patrons of these establishments may not be able to negotiate mutually agreeable outcomes, it does not mean that a market mechanism does not exist.

Exactly what is *public* about a restaurant or bar? If a restaurant is privately owned, there may be nothing at all about it that is public. Granted, restaurants allow complete strangers to come in off the street and be customers, but the decisions made by the restaurants with respect to menu, atmosphere, opening and closing times, and so on, are strictly privately determined. Of course, restaurants are subject to all sorts of social controls involving health and safety issues, and the state can impose smoking bans, but the point I want to make is that a market mechanism does exist to deal with secondhand smoke. The mechanism may not be perfect, and ultimately social control may be warranted, but I believe the market mechanism is worth considering.

A private restaurant relies on its customers to stay in business and make profit. Probably the most important decisions a restaurant makes involve the menu and the prices, but location, parking, atmosphere, and other factors affect patronage. A restaurant that does not allow smoking may be unattractive to smokers. A restaurant that allows smoking may be unattractive to nonsmokers. A restaurant that has a separate smoking section may be able to strike a balance between smokers and nonsmokers.

The restaurant business is generally highly competitive. Restaurant owners can compete for customers across many dimensions. If the smoking policy is a key competitive weapon, the market may easily sort itself out by naturally allowing for restaurants to simultaneously exist with different smoking policies in place. Smokers and nonsmokers can decide which restaurants to choose based on whatever criteria they deem important.

One study uses survey data collected from restaurants and bars in Genesee County, Michigan, in 2009, when there were no state smoking bans in place. Thus, these establishments were able to determine their own smoking policies. The main results of the study were that the vast majority of these establishments (87 percent) did voluntarily establish smoking rules, but the rules varied based on the type of establishment. Most of the restaurants that did not have bars chose to ban smoking outright. Most of the restaurants that did have bars restricted smoking to the bar area or to a well-ventilated separate area. These results suggest that a secondhand smoke market response does exist that caters to different customer bases.

So, is a restaurant deciding upon a smoking policy any different than a restaurant deciding whether to serve only meat dishes, only vegetarian dishes, or a mixture of the two? Most people would say of course it is: menu items can't kill you! Is it all, then, a matter of the *degree* of the externality? Is banning smoking in restaurants warranted because smoking is dangerous to nonsmokers? Let's take an extreme position and say that secondhand smoke instantly kills nonsmokers. Even in this case, social intervention may not be necessary, because market forces would likely give restaurant owners strong incentives to ban smoking. But if restaurant owners still refused to ban smoking, would social intervention now be warranted? Maybe not.

I have a friend who is a serious antismoking advocate. My friend loves music, especially live music in venues like bars. Unfortunately, he is extremely asthmatic and can't survive in a smoky bar for more than a few minutes. He once offered me a very compelling argument as to why smoking in bars should be banned. If the main attractions of going to a bar are drinking, listening to music, and socializing with other patrons, a nonsmoker who is severely bothered by smoke cannot enjoy all these activities. However, a smoker still can enjoy these activities but cannot smoke while enjoying them. Smoking will have to be done outside or not at all. Thus, allowing smoking excludes some patrons from all of the main activities a bar has to offer, but banning smoking only prevents customers from smoking while in a bar. This argument not only appears to justify banning smoking in bars, it elegantly appeals to common sense. But it still does not definitively resolve the debate.

Any externality requires the participation of at least two parties—the polluter and the victim. Although the polluter bears the burden of being the one who actively creates the pollution, the victim must actually be affected for an externality to exist. This suggests that there can be at least two crude ways of preventing an externality: one way is to prevent the polluter from polluting; the other way is to relocate the victim. If all the people who are bothered by secondhand smoke don't go to restaurants or bars that allow smoking, there will be no negative externalities in those venues. The cost of that behavior is the lost value from not being able to patronize certain restaurants and bars. Banning smoking, on the other hand, also eliminates the externality, but at the cost of the lost value to smokers who will not be able to smoke at will. Determining which lost value is greater can be an extremely difficult thing to do.

One common criticism often raised against smoking bans in restaurants and bars is that the policy could reduce the profitability of these establishments. When there is a movement to encourage smoking ban policies, this criticism is usually carefully addressed. Consider the organization Clean Air Kansas (www.cleanairkansas.org) that had the goal of a statewide smoking ban covering indoor public places and workplaces, including bars, restaurants, and private clubs. As part of its campaign, it addressed the argument that smoke-free policies would harm businesses by publishing a succinct summary of some studies on the issue. Here are the points it presented:

1. A study of sales tax data from 81 localities in six states found that smoke-free ordinances have no effect on revenues.

2. Studying the quality and funding sources of 97 reports on the economic impact of smoke-free policies, researchers concluded that all the best-designed studies report that smoke-free restaurant and bar laws have no impact or a positive impact on sales or employment.

3. Studies that used objective measures such as sales tax receipts, included data from several years before and after, and controlled for changes in economic conditions found no negative economic impact from smoke-free policies.

4. Researchers found that studies showing negative impacts on the hospitality industry were usually based on predictions or estimates of changes. Mainly funded by the tobacco industry, none were published in peer-reviewed journals.

Although these above points understate it, there is a legitimate empirical debate on whether smoking bans increase or reduce the profitability of restaurants and bars. As usual, the evidence is mixed. Furthermore, studies that determine the profitability of smoking bans must, by necessity, deal with *average* outcomes. This means that not all establishments will benefit. Furthermore, it is interesting that some establishments prefer not to comply with the bans and instead pay the fines that are levied against them. For these establishments, that is fairly compelling evidence that they do not find their profitability has increased because of the bans. Nevertheless, I want to focus on a slightly different issue. Let's say it is true that smoking bans unambiguously improve restaurant and bar profitability. The question I would like to address is this: Does this strengthen or weaken the argument for social policy control?

As discussed in the last chapter, when social policy is motivated, at least in part, by the argument that the state knows what is best for private individuals, does the policy make the individuals better off? If it is true that restaurants and bars can increase their profits by banning smoking, why does the state need to mandate smoking bans? The studies that show how profitable smoking bans can be should be persuasive in their own right. Maybe restaurant and bar owners simply didn't understand the value of smoking bans to their own bottom lines. But once they are properly informed, they can then decide for themselves how best to proceed. One more point: If the social goal is to truly protect nonsmokers from secondhand smoke, then what does it matter what happens to restaurant and bar profitability? Lost profits would simply be a cost of the policy, offset by the benefits of reducing exposure to ETS.

Yet another argument for banning smoking, especially in bars, is to protect the *employees* of these establishments, as opposed to protecting the nonsmoking patrons. This is a clever argument that has been the driving force behind several antismoking initiatives. One may accept the argument that nonsmoking customers can refuse to patronize establishments that allow smoking, but when it comes to employees there often is a sense that these workers are somehow trapped in their jobs. If workers are forced to inhale secondhand smoke, they are adversely affected at no fault of their own.

The problem with this argument is that there is no compelling reason that workers who are unsatisfied with certain job conditions can't find other jobs. Secondhand smoke is only one aspect of working conditions. Employees must consider salary, hours, medical and retirement packages, vacation time, job risks, and several other factors when determining the attractiveness of a job. My antismoking friend couldn't work in a bar because of his asthma, so he became an accomplished scholar instead. In his case, maybe it was a good thing that the bars in Montreal never banned smoking.

Along similar lines, consider the incentives of an owner of a restaurant, or bar, or any other work establishment for that matter. If you own a business, you want your employees to be productive. If you have smoking and nonsmoking employees at odds with each other, this may hurt your business. But this can be a private matter. Just as a restaurant owner can try to determine the best smoking policy for customers, an employer can determine the best smoking policy for workers. This policy may involve a complete ban at the workplace, or special smoking areas, or nothing at all, but there exists a market mechanism that can deal with the issue of smoking at the workplace.

One final side note about justifying smoking bans to protect employees. In the Michigan survey discussed above, the authors found that the vast majority of employees in bars and restaurants did not complain about secondhand smoke, especially since a large number of them were smokers themselves. Thus, it could very well be that allowing smoking in certain venues *attracts* employees who smoke to those jobs. Thus, smoking bans do not create a win-win situation for everyone impacted by the ban. The market mechanism may not work perfectly, and social intervention may be useful in dealing with ETS, but the main point I am trying to make is that social intervention is not *necessarily* required to handle the negative externality of secondhand smoke in "public" places.

DOES DEATH DESERVE SOME CREDIT?

If you were to compare the medical costs incurred by a smoker and a nonsmoker, the evidence is clear that a smoker has higher medical costs. However, on average, smokers live six to eight fewer years than nonsmokers. So, from a lifetime perspective, smokers may incur fewer costs involving nursing home care, pension payments, and social security payments. So how do economists use this fact to upset people? Let me just get this out of the way quickly: from a financial perspective, the early death of smokers may be providing a *benefit* in terms of savings on certain costs.

The concept of a financial savings, or *death credit*, that smokers yield because of their lower life expectancy is extremely controversial. When individual states began pursuing lawsuits against the tobacco companies in the mid-1990s, the argument justifying the damages sought was a simple one: tobacco makes people ill; the states, through Medicaid, incur expenses to care for the ill; and the tobacco companies should be responsible for these expenses. But what if the overall expenses incurred by smokers fall short of the expenses incurred by nonsmokers? What then are the financial damages suffered by the states due to tobacco?

When the idea of a death credit was initially raised, it was greeted with such words as *ghoulish, repugnant,* and *immoral.* But let me recast the idea of a death credit in a way that may make it seem more plausible. Assume you are bearing the financial responsibility of caring for an elderly relative who resides in a private nursing home. There comes a time when, sadly, your relative passes away. At that point, however, the nursing home continues to bill you for six more years. It is unlikely that you are going to be willing to pay for six more years of costs that are never incurred by the nursing home. Please keep in mind that I am not claiming that you are better off because your relative passed away. You may gladly have been willing to incur six more years of expenses to take care of your relative. But there is no denying that your financial burden was eased at the passing of your relative. Does that really seem ghoulish to you?

There have been several studies that have attempted to estimate the financial costs smokers impose on society, and there has been a fair amount of disagreement as to what should be included in the analysis and how the estimation should be conducted. I'm going to focus on one approach that has attempted to estimate the *differential* financial insurance costs, per pack of cigarettes, between smokers and nonsmokers. (A positive differential cost implies smokers are more costly; a negative differential cost implies they are less costly.) For my purposes, I'd like to illustrate how the concept of a death credit can enter into this estimation without going into the minute details of how the estimation is conducted.

If you compare the lifetime insurance costs of smokers and non-smokers, what are the main items that can be included that lead to higher costs for smokers? First, there are total medical care costs. Smoking definitely adversely affects the health of smokers and leads to higher medical costs. Second, there are group life insurance costs. With a shorter expected life span, the inclusion of smokers in life insurance pools increases the premiums that must be paid. Third, again because of their shorter life span, smokers contribute less in earning taxes, such as social security taxes to the government. If you add all these differential costs up, that indicates the excess financial costs smokers impose on society relative to nonsmokers.

But what about the benefit side of the story? There are two main components in which smokers are likely to have lower insurance costs than nonsmokers. First, their lower life expectancy leads to lower nursing home costs. Second, many smokers die before they reclaim money from retirement and pension plans, or they die before much is reclaimed. Nonsmokers can be more costly to finance with these types of plans. If you add these benefits together, you get the death credit, which is likely to be a negative dollar amount that indicates the excess financial benefits smokers impose on society relative to nonsmokers.

When you put the costs and benefits together, it is possible that they sum to a negative dollar amount. If this is the case, one could argue that smoking is, in effect, a self-financing activity. Smokers are *less* of a financial drain on society than are nonsmokers. But it could also easily be the other way around: the costs may outweigh the benefits. Both outcomes have been supported by the available evidence.

Unfortunately, there is no consensus on how to conduct this type of study. How are the dollar amounts calculated? Should taxes on cigarettes be considered as part of the financial benefits smokers impose on society? Should there be a broader view of the costs and benefits? For example, should the studies include secondhand smoke costs or the lost value of human life? Some argue that the original lawsuits brought by individual states only considered the financial insurance costs to the states as appropriate damages. If this is true, it may be incorrect to include broader concepts of costs and benefits for the purposes of that particular legal issue. Whatever the case, it must be made clear that the cost-benefit analysis being done is either a narrow insurance one or a more encompassing social one. Both types of analyses are legitimate, but they answer different questions.

However you feel about these studies, the key point I am trying to make is that the concept of a death credit is important. If it is excluded from the analysis, the net financial costs of smoking are going to be inaccurate. If it is included, there is a possibility, but not a guarantee, that cigarettes can be found to be self-financing. If one criticism is that smokers impose a financial drain on society due to excessive insurance costs, the death credit may reduce the impact of that criticism.

One last point about the death credit. Recently, I was lecturing on the pros and cons of developing a market for the selling of organs for transplant. I asked my students if they could think of some of the benefits of developing such a market. One student quickly answered that a market would increase the supply of organs relative to what exists now. Before I could respond, another student surprised me by saying that increasing the supply of organs may be a bad thing to do. When I asked her why, she responded by saying that there is a benefit to society if people die young, just as I discussed about smoking and the death credit. Well, at least one student was paying attention during that lecture.

I am not claiming that death is a good thing. Not at all. But trade-offs exist everywhere, even in death. If one is trying to argue that the states are incurring an excessive financial burden by taking care of sick smokers, it is a fact that the burden is lessened when smokers die. It is also a fact that smokers die younger than nonsmokers but not due to social intervention. Remember, smoking is a *choice*, not a requirement. You may believe that it is not a well-informed choice, or that smokers are addicted, or that other factors that I discussed in the previous chapter are at work, but no one is actually forcing smokers to smoke just so they can die young.

SEARCHING FOR THE TRUTH

In 2006, the Surgeon General's Office released a report titled *The Health Consequences of Involuntary Exposure to Tobacco Smoke*. The report painstakingly catalogs the health impact of secondhand smoke found in numerous studies. While the full report is over 700 pages long, fortunately there is a very brief summary of six of its major conclusions:

1. Many millions of Americans, both children and adults, are still exposed to secondhand smoke in their homes and workplaces despite substantial progress in tobacco control.
2. Secondhand smoke exposure causes disease and premature death in children and adults who do not smoke.
3. Children exposed to secondhand smoke are at an increased risk for sudden infant death syndrome (SIDS), acute respiratory infections, ear problems, and more severe asthma. Smoking by parents causes respiratory symptoms and slows lung growth in their children.
4. Exposure of adults to secondhand smoke has immediate adverse effects on the cardiovascular system and causes coronary heart disease and lung cancer.
5. The scientific evidence indicates that there is no risk-free level of exposure to secondhand smoke.
6. Eliminating smoking in indoor spaces fully protects nonsmokers from exposure to secondhand smoke. Separating smokers from nonsmokers, cleaning the air, and ventilating buildings cannot eliminate exposures of nonsmokers to secondhand smoke.

In light of this mountain of evidence, how could anyone challenge this simple conclusion: secondhand smoke leads to severe adverse health outcomes in nonsmokers.

When I give public lectures on the economics of smoking, I usually find a poor (and sometimes hostile) response to two points I like to make: the costs of secondhand smoke may be overstated, and the benefits of secondhand smoke are definitely understated. Ignoring the fact that I make these points specifically to rile people up, let me elaborate as to why I believe these points deserve careful consideration, especially from a public policy perspective.

When undertaking an empirical study to determine the health impact of secondhand smoke, there are many complicating issues that need to be addressed. First, the cleanest way to measure the impact of secondhand smoke is to compare those who have been exposed to ETS to a control group of people who haven't been exposed. Unfortunately, unless you corral a group of people from birth and make sure they are never exposed to ETS, that particular control group would be very difficult to identify, if it even exists.

Second, there is an old saying among professional poisoners: *the dose makes the poison.* Exposure to ETS is often measured by survey questions, but simply knowing if someone is exposed to ETS and for how long the exposure lasts is not enough information to determine precisely the biological impact on health. Take a deep breath wherever you are right now. I assure you, you are sucking in some dangerous chemicals, none of which are likely to be at a high enough dose to cause you any harm, now or in the long run (although it does depend on *where* you are right now, so ignore my claim if you are working with toxic chemicals and not wearing a protective mask). Although biologically effective doses of ETS are very difficult to measure, the surgeon general's report does discuss the importance of using *biomarkers* to provide additional validity to the survey responses. The most common biomarker is *cotinine*:

> Cotinine is the major metabolite (breakdown product) of nicotine. Exposure to nicotine can be measured by analyzing the cotinine level in the blood, saliva, or urine. Since nicotine is highly specific to tobacco smoke, serum cotinine levels track exposure to tobacco smoke and its toxic constituents. Cotinine assays provide an objective quantitative measure that is more reliable than smoking histories or counting the number of cigarettes smoked per day. Cotinine also permits the measurement of exposure to second-hand smoke (passive smoking). (MedicineNet.com)

There are other biomarkers, and while they also have shortcomings as to how precisely they can link ETS exposure to adverse health outcomes, they do provide a useful measure for researchers to consider.

Third, even with the benefits of using biomarkers to measure ETS exposure, survey data is very commonly used to provide researchers with exposure data. It's simply more pragmatic to ask several thousand people about their smoking behavior and exposure to secondhand smoke than it is to take blood, saliva or urine samples. I have often asked my students to participate in class by answering survey questions, but I can't see myself sending them to the bathroom to pee in a cup. While survey data is phenomenally important and useful, their major shortcoming is that of reliability. Even completely sincere respondents may not accurately recall the correct information. For example, if a study is interested in the cumulative effects of lifetime smoking and respondents are between the ages of 60 and 70, how accurately can they answer questions about when they started smoking and how often they smoked throughout their entire lives, how often they were exposed to ETS and under what conditions, and so on? And what about the respondents who actually lie?

Fourth, there can be a variety of confounding factors that make it very difficult to attribute an adverse health outcome specifically to ETS exposure. Are people who are exposed to ETS also exposed to other possible carcinogens? What are their lifestyle choices in terms of diet and exercise? Do they have genetic propensities for certain diseases? Again, the surgeon general's report discusses the importance of confounding factors, but even studies that attempt to take these into account may not be able to identify all the relevant ones, let alone collect the appropriate data.

Finally, despite the strong conclusions offered in the surgeon general's report, there have been a number of studies (acknowledged in the report) of the risks associated with ETS exposure that have led to highly conflicting results. For example, in terms of ETS exposure increasing the risk of developing lung cancer, there are studies that can be found to support each of three possible outcomes: ETS increases the risk, has no impact on the risk, or decreases the risk. These eclectic results are likely due to the complicating issues I have just identified, and they demonstrate one important point: saying that studies like these *prove* a result is far too strong a statement.

Where does all this leave us concerning the costs of secondhand smoke? The fact that the scientific evidence on the health risks of exposure to ETS is far from conclusive, and that the studies that do find such risks have to deal with a laundry list of potential problems, does not mean that there are no health risks to ETS. Personally, I have no problem believing there can be substantial risks associated with ETS exposure in certain settings, but me saying that and the government devoting hundreds of millions of dollars of resources in designing and implementing policy controls are two entirely different matters.

For some researchers, finding evidence of the adverse health effects of ETS exposure is where the analysis begins and ends. If such evidence exists, the public policy debate then focuses on which policies to implement, not on whether there is sense in implementing any at all. To some economists, like myself, determining whether ETS is dangerous is not the key policy issue. Let's hypothetically say that there is definitive evidence that exposure to ETS poses absolutely no health risks. Does this mean there are no social costs associated with ETS? Not at all.

Secondhand smoke may bother people who don't like the smell of smoke getting into their clothes, or hair, or ruining their enjoyment of a meal in a restaurant. These may sound like trivial costs compared to increased risks of developing cancer, but they need to be considered in the proper context. Certainly, the per incident cost of being bothered by secondhand smoke may be small, not much more than an annoyance, but it is a cost that occurs *every time* you are exposed to ETS. If you work with people who smoke, these small daily annoyances can quickly add up week after week and month after month. Small costs that occur with high frequency may, cumulatively, very well outweigh huge costs that occur with low frequency. The point is, economists tend to consider *all* the external costs of an activity they can identify. If ETS turned out not to be a health issue after all, I can still imagine economists discussing the public policy implications of controlling secondhand smoke to prevent other costs.

There is the other side of the story also. Let's say ETS exposure turns out to unambiguously cause adverse health outcomes. Does this mean that the next step is to consider which policy controls to implement? Not at all. And this is where the benefits of secondhand smoke can be introduced. At first blush, it seems utterly ridiculous to speak of benefits nonsmokers reap from having cigarette smoke blown into their faces. But those are not the benefits I am identifying. Secondhand smoke, like most examples of pollution, is the byproduct of a productive activity. Think of an airport that has noisy landing patterns that disturb neighboring residents. The noise pollution is the byproduct of the productive activity of having air travel. The airports aren't purposely landing planes with no goal other than to bother the residents. When factories produce goods, air pollution may be a problem. The costs of the pollution, then, must be weighed against the benefits of the productive activity. There may be a role for social policy to achieve some optimal balance, but there may not be such a role.

If there are substantial costs to ETS exposure, these costs can still be weighed against the benefits smokers receive from smoking. As discussed at the beginning of the previous chapter, that benefits to smoking exist is a fact, not an opinion. How you want to count these benefits in a social welfare calculation is another matter. But this is where I believe economists can have a very different perspective on an issue like ETS than many other scholars. It really isn't surprising to identify an activity that imposes costs upon others. There are countless examples of negative externalities. The interesting aspect of dealing with a negative externality is to determine what is the best way to trade-off the costs and the benefits of the activity. Can the market take care of the problem? Is the solution to use policy intervention, and if so, exactly what type of intervention?

Often when I talk about the benefits of smoking, I am accused of ignoring the costs. As an economist, I try to take into account *all* the trade-offs I can identify. When I identify some benefits that may not be obvious to others, it is to eventually weigh them against the costs. Likewise, when I identify some costs that may not be obvious to others, it is to eventually weigh them against the benefits.

There is one further aspect of the empirical research on ETS exposure that I would like to discuss. In May 2003, the *British Medical Journal* published a study that found no adverse health effects of ETS. The study was conducted by two epidemiologists, and their results drew immediate attention from antismoking groups. The harshest criticism, however, was not about the technical merits of the study. The criticism focused on the following footnote:

> In recent years JEE [one of the authors] has received funds originating from the tobacco industry for his tobacco related epidemiological research because it has been impossible for him to obtain equivalent funds from other sources. GCK [the other author] never received funds from the tobacco industry until last year, when he conducted an epidemiological review for a law firm which has several tobacco companies as clients.

The authors were criticized for being pawns of the tobacco industry, and as a result, the critics argued that their findings should be dismissed.

I have never been impressed with this type of criticism for any empirical study, not because it isn't valid but because it is *always* valid. Research that is funded by outside interests can always be tainted, *regardless* of which side of the issue the results support. Many studies that find adverse health effects of ETS are funded by such groups as the World Health Organization, the National Cancer Institute, the Environmental Protection Agency, and other organizations with possible vested interests in certain results. Researchers who are funded by these groups can just as easily be criticized for being influenced by their backers.

More fundamentally, even without outside funding, can you ever be sure of the motives behind *any* research agenda? Any researcher can have a personal agenda that may push the results in a particular direction. Also, studies that find no significant results may be less interesting for editors of academic journals to publish, also creating pressure to find "certain" types of results. But does any of this really matter?

As I discussed in chapter 1, the important aspects of empirical work have to do with the integrity of the data, the ability to replicate results, and the robustness of the results to different statistical approaches. There will always be sincere disagreements as to what data and statistical techniques are appropriate to use, and I believe these are the issues that can most constructively be debated. There will also always be researchers who struggle with keeping their biases under control. That is the nature of empirical research.

I honestly have no idea if the costs of smoking grossly exceed the benefits, or vice versa. It may be sound social policy to reduce the consumption of cigarettes, and maybe even to completely ban them. On the other hand, it may be sound social policy to pull back on some of the current antismoking regulations. On whichever side of the debate you find yourself, I believe that a good understanding of *all* the trade-offs associated with smoking can only lead to better-informed policy decisions.

An intense antismoking friend of mine once expressed his viewpoint on smoking quite simply. He supports a complete ban on smoking because he sincerely believes it is the best social solution. How could I argue against that position? I did, however, ask him to accept the premise that the best outcome is not truly known. What policy option would he choose in that case? His response was that he would err on the side of health and safety and still recommend a complete ban. I disagreed with him. My response was that I would err on the side of personal freedom and let individuals and restaurant and bar owners decide for themselves how best to deal with the smoking issue. What I didn't tell him, however, is that if he had said he would err on the side of personal freedom, I would have convincingly said that I would err on the side of health and safety. That is why I love being an economist—I'm trained to be disagreeable. Then again, maybe I was born disagreeable and that is why I became an economist.

NOTES

The two sunlight cases cited are Fontainebleau Hotel Corp. v. Forty-Five Twenty-Five Inc., 114 So. 2d 357 (1959); and Prah v. Maretti, 108 Wis. 2d 223 (1982).

The seminal work on social costs and property rights is by Ronald Coase, "The Problem of Social Cost," *Journal of Law and Economics* 3 (1960): 1–44. The topic of negative externalities is always well covered in any law and economics text, such as Robert Cooter and Thomas Ulen, *Law and Economics*, 6th ed. (Boston, MA: Addison Wesley, 2012).

The article that uses the survey data from Michigan is Amelia Biehl and Christopher C. Douglas, "How Do Private Markets Address Smoking Externalities?" *Journal of Economics* 37 (2011): 39–57.

A few accessible articles on secondhand smoke and smoking bans are Michael L. Marlow, "The Economic Losers from Smoking Bans," *Regulation* 33 (2010) 14–19; Thomas A. Lambert, "The Case against Smoking Bans," *Regulation* 29 (2006): 34–40; and Gio Batta Gori, "Stoking the Rigged Terror of Secondhand Smoke," *Regulation* 30 (2007): 14–17. An empirical study about smoking bans and restaurant profitability is by Benjamin C. Alamar and Stanton A. Glanz, "Smoke-Free Ordinances Increase Restaurant Profit and Value," *Contemporary Economic Policy* 22 (2004): 520–25.

For a fascinating historical perspective on antismoking policies, see Robert N. Proctor, "The Anti-Tobacco Campaign of the Nazis: A Little Known Aspect of Public Health in Germany, 1933–45," *British Medical Journal* 313 (1996): 1450–53.

W. Kip Viscusi offers an extensive discussion of the social costs of smoking in *Smoke-Filled Rooms* (Chicago: University of Chicago Press, 2002). A much shorter and more accessible piece of his is "Secondhand Smoke: Facts and Fantasy," *Regulation* 18 (1995): 42–49.

Viscusi's work is controversial, and there are several sources that critique his approach or take a different one. For example, see Maribeth Coller, Glenn W. Harrison, and Melayne Morgan McInnes, "Evaluating the Tobacco Settlement Damage Awards: Too Much or Not Enough?" *American Journal of Public Health* 92 (2002): 1–6; David M. Cutler et al., "How Good a Deal Was the Tobacco Settlement? Assessing Payments to Massachusetts," *Journal of Risk and Uncertainty* 21 (2000): 235–61; and especially, Jon D. Hanson and Kyle D. Logue, "The Cost of Cigarettes: The Economic Case for Ex Post Incentive-Based Regulation," *Yale Law Journal* 107 (1998): 1163–1361.

The citation for the surgeon general's report is US Department of Health and Human Services, *The Health Consequences of Involuntary Exposure to Tobacco Smoke: A Report of the Surgeon General—Executive Summary* (2006).

The article that found no adverse health effects of ETS is by James E. Enstrom and Geoffrey C. Kabat, "Environmental Tobacco Smoke and Tobacco Related Mortality in a Prospective Study of Californians, 1960–98," *British Medical Journal* 326 (2003): 1057–66. Also see the editorial that precedes the article.

7   *Behave Yourself*

HAVE YOU EVER driven a rental car? There is something so liberating about driving someone else's car, especially when you have complete insurance coverage. The parking space that might be a bit of a tight fit no longer worries you. The 72-ounce super drink that doesn't quite fit in the beverage holder no longer distracts you. You don't have to worry about using cheap gas, squealing the tires, or slamming on the brakes. Driving a rental car is a pleasure.

You may be thinking to yourself that no responsible adult would ever abuse a rental car in those ways, at least not on purpose. You may be right, but let me restate the issue. Have you ever loaned your car to someone? What goes through your mind when you do? Do you give the driver a list of instructions to make sure that person takes good care of your car? Or do you just quietly worry about your car being mishandled? Do you have a slight feeling of hesitation just as you hand over the car keys? If you answered yes to these questions, you have a good idea of what I'm getting at. People tend to take better care with their own property than they would with someone else's property. Ownership in and of itself can affect behavior. If you doubt that statement, just ask landlords what they think, especially in a college town.

Economists have their own way of thinking about behavior in some settings. In this chapter, I'm going to present a series of examples of some of these settings. The main point that I want to get across to you is one you often get from a *Twilight Zone* episode: *things are not always what they seem to be.*

BUCKLE UP FOR SAFETY, OR MAYBE NOT

Wearing a seat belt seems like such an obvious safety feature for drivers to adopt. If you wear a seat belt and are in an accident, the risk of being seriously injured goes down. Thus, when you wear a seat belt, you feel safer. This feeling of security, however, may actually lead you to drive more carelessly. In effect, the costs of driving carelessly have decreased, so you drive more carelessly. Many people are skeptical about this line of reasoning. It's quite reasonable to disbelieve that your driving behavior will be affected by wearing a seat belt, but it's not any single individual's behavior that matters. There may be many people who truly don't drive any differently when wearing a seat belt, but the argument may hold true for some drivers. If that is the case, mandatory seat belt laws have the potential to actually *increase* the accident rate. Drivers may be relatively safer if an accident occurs, but other passengers, pedestrians, bicyclists, and motorcyclists may be less safe. This effect is known as *offsetting behavior*. The technological safety aspects of seat belts may be offset by the behavioral responses of drivers being more careless.

As a more extreme example, do you ever watch those wild police chase videos on television? There's one I particularly enjoy. It involves a man getting into a tank and driving through residential areas. The images of people standing on their front lawns and watching a tank crush their parked cars are priceless. Now that is serious offsetting behavior. That man felt very safe in the tank and, as a result, drove more carelessly.

When I ask people who wear seat belts whether they drive more carelessly and they say they don't, I like to rephrase the question: "What would you do if the next time you got into your car, the seat belt was broken and you couldn't wear it?" Often times, people respond by saying that they would drive more carefully until the seat belt was repaired. Doesn't that imply they would drive *less carefully* when the seat belt was not broken? One economist once offered a different way to improve driving safety—take a very sharp stake and mount it into the steering wheel column with the point just one inch from the driver's heart. That ought to encourage safer driving.

THE SUN AND I

Have you ever been annoyed by those television commercials for local news that go something like this: "A new study finds a common household item to be deadly; tune in at eleven for all the details, along with sports and tomorrow's weather update." One day, one of those commercials caught my attention: "A new study finds that sunblock increases your chance of getting skin cancer; tune in at eleven and we'll give you the details." That worried me because I had just started wearing sunblock to *lower* my chance of getting skin cancer. It was just my luck that after years of supposedly being reckless with my health, I took a precaution that turned out to be a carcinogen.

As the day wore on, I started to think about this problem a bit more carefully. I began to seriously doubt that the sunblock I was using was, in and of itself, a carcinogen. Then I figured out what the study must be about. When people wear sunblock, they may get the feeling that they are protected from the sun for hours on end. I guessed the study was going to demonstrate offsetting behavior: wearing sunblock was increasing individuals' exposure to sun, negating the effect of the sunblock. When I tuned in at eleven, that is exactly what the story was about. I was, however, taken by surprise with the latest weather update. The next day was going to be hot and sunny. They recommended wearing sunblock if you were going to be outside.

HOCKEY NIGHT IN CANADA

If you grew up in Canada, the expression *Hockey Night in Canada* is well known to you. Every Saturday night during the hockey season, a hockey game was shown on television. If you lived in Montreal in the

1970s, which I did, you had the privilege of sharing your city with the greatest hockey team in the world at that time—the Montreal Canadians. Unfortunately, I was a Boston Bruins fan. The one-time coach of the Bruins, Don Cherry, made a controversial prediction back in 1979. In a recent interview, he reflected on that prediction:

> In the old days, we never thought of hitting anyone headfirst into the boards. Never! In 1979 when they put helmets on and all got protected, I predicted you would have head injuries like you wouldn't believe because guys took more liberties hitting one another. We have more concussions now in a week than we used to have in a year. (*Reader's Digest Canadian Edition*, March 2003, 64–65)

Don Cherry clearly understood the concept of offsetting behavior. If you require an athlete in a contact sport to wear more protective equipment, that will make the athlete safer only if it doesn't affect the behavior of the players. Protected players feel safer and, therefore, can be more aggressive. Also, if your rivals are more protected, you may feel you can't hurt them as easily, so you are not as worried about hitting them. This is exactly the seat belt phenomenon applied to contact sports. It can also apply to protective equipment for skateboarding, bicycling, rollerblading, and other potentially dangerous activities. You may think you are protecting your children by making them wear protective equipment, but you may actually be increasing their chances of injury if they become more daring.

SAFE FOR CHILDREN, IF NOT FOR THE ADULTS

Child poisoning is a serious problem. In the early 1970s, the Consumer Product Safety Commission (CPSC) had the extremely good intention of protecting children by enforcing child safety cap regulations, especially for common household items like aspirin. Safety caps make it difficult, but not impossible, for children to remove the caps and ingest the medicine. How can anyone argue against the CPSC's safety caps regulation? I'll give it a try.

There appear to be two offsetting behavioral problems with safety cap regulation for aspirin. First, because adults feel that the safety caps are technically effective and cannot be opened by children, they may tend to leave unopened bottles in plain view. Without the safety caps, many adults may leave aspirin locked away, or at least out of plain sight. With the safety caps, there may be a tendency to leave the aspirin on a bathroom or kitchen counter. This easier access to the aspirin can lead to more child poisoning if the caps do not completely prevent child tampering. Second, safety caps can be difficult to open for some adults, especially ones who have arthritis or other pains in their hands, and this may increase the tendency for these individuals not to always replace the caps. In this case, there may be more poisonings from open bottles. Thus, offsetting behavior can work against the desired goal of the safety cap regulation. Increased safety is not solely a technical problem; it is also a problem of how people behave with technical safeguards.

HAZARDOUS TO YOUR MORALS

Most people have some form of insurance for something or other. You may insure your health, car, home, property, and other things that are valuable to you. Insurance allows you to pay a premium to cover a potential loss that can substantially outweigh the premium. For example, you buy car insurance for $500 a year. If at the end of the year you had the good fortune not to have an accident and make a claim, you don't get your $500 refunded. But if you were in an accident, your insurance company would pay for damages that could be in the thousands of dollars. Insurance companies can survive because they keep all the premiums paid to them and only pay out when accidents occur. The premiums, then, are largely determined by the probabilities that accidents occur and by the amount of losses that the insurance companies have to pay out. (Premiums also depend on the costs of operating an insurance company, but this won't be of primary importance for what I want to discuss.)

Let's say that theft coverage is included as part of your $500 car insurance premium. If your car is stolen, your insurance company will reimburse you the *full* current value of your car. In other words, if your car is stolen and you have insurance, in a sense you still own the same car. The probability that your car is stolen can depend on many things—where you live, whether you park in a garage, the type of car you drive, and so on. Insurance companies spend a great deal of time determining these types of probabilities because they are an integral part of setting premiums. However, one complication that insurance companies face is that the selling of insurance in and of itself may affect the probability of a loss occurring.

An insurance company pays attention to many things when you buy insurance. Where you live and what type of car you drive are two of them. Whether you park in a garage, however, may not be one of them. If not, the insurance company may face a problem known as *moral hazard*. Assume that you can lower the probability of your car being stolen if you park it in a garage. The sensible thing to do, then, may be to park in a garage. But parking in a garage may be costly to you, either because of the parking fee you may have to pay or even because of the bother of getting in and out of a garage. If you are fully covered for the loss of your car in case of theft, what benefit would you get from parking in a garage? If the car is stolen, you will be fully compensated. So, for some positive cost of protecting your car, you receive no additional benefit. The full insurance, in effect, alters your incentive to take care of your car. This is the moral hazard problem: the insurance coverage changes the way you behave and increases the probability of your car being stolen.

There are two key factors behind moral hazard. The first involves an *unobservable action*. If the insurance company can observe all actions that affect the probability of an accident, your insurance premium can be adjusted to reflect your behavior. The more care you take to lower the probability of an accident, the lower will be your premium. If your insurance company requires you to park in a garage to be compensated for a loss, there will be no moral hazard problem. You may decide not to buy the theft insurance if you feel parking in a garage is an unreasonable condition, or you may have to buy insurance at a higher premium. But if you insure, your premium will depend on your actions.

The second important factor behind moral hazard is the concept of *full insurance*. Even if the insurance company fully compensates you for the value of your car, are you really *fully* insured if your car is stolen? There will be other costs you incur that are not insurable, such as your time costs of dealing with the loss, your frustration, the inconvenience of having to find substitute transportation, the bother of buying a new car, and so forth. To the extent that you have to bear part of the risk of your car being stolen, the moral hazard problem will be mitigated.

Along the same lines, insurance companies are well aware of the moral hazard problem. Quite often, insurance is not meant to provide full coverage. Deductibles are one way to allow a person buying insurance to bear some risk. Coinsurance (or partial coverage) is another way. If an insurance company is dealing with an unobservable action like keeping the car in a garage, but it realizes the individual is not purchasing full coverage, that may be enough information to satisfy the insurance company that the action will be taken after all. As long as the individual is bearing enough risk to affect behavior, an unobservable action may still be taken.

Moral hazard has the potential to affect all types of insurance. One common criticism of socialized health insurance is that medical resources will be wasted because of the moral hazard problem. People who don't bear the full risk of their actions may not take appropriate care of their health. Obviously, most people are not going to purposely allow their health to degenerate because they have full health insurance. But on the margin, there may be some people who worry less about the risks of smoking or drinking, or about the benefits of diet and exercise.

For example, while health insurance plans traditionally provided stronger coverage for physical ailments than for mental illnesses and addiction treatments, in the 1980s and 1990s many states enacted parity mandates. These mandates required insurance plans to provide similar coverage for physical as well as mental illnesses. One economic study examined whether this more comprehensive coverage would affect current alcohol consumption by reducing future addiction treatment costs. Comparing states that adopted the parity mandate to those that didn't, the study found that there is an impact on behavior—per capita beer consumption increased by approximately 14 percent in the states with enhanced coverage but did not increase in the other states. It may not be clear whether this increase in beer consumption had a huge impact on the amount of resources used in addiction treatments, but it does demonstrate how insurance coverage can affect behavior.

Another study examines the impact of the US Medicare system (social health insurance for seniors age 65 or older) on the behavior of men. Specifically, the study looks at two groups of men *before* the age of 65—those who have health insurance and those who do not—and then examines the impact of Medicare on their behavior *after* the age of 65. The idea is simple: if you had health insurance before age 65, your behavior should not be much affected by continuing to have health insurance through Medicare after age 65; but if you were uninsured before age 65, the Medicare insurance after age 65 has the potential to create moral hazard problems. The study finds some evidence that Medicare does have strong behavioral impacts, finding that men new to health insurance are less likely to engage in vigorous physical activity, less likely to quit smoking, and more likely to drink alcohol.

While these and other studies do provide evidence that health insurance has to contend with moral hazard problems, there are also many studies that do not support such a finding. When it comes to health, individuals are rarely fully insured. Bad health outcomes create losses that often well exceed the insurable medical costs or lost wages. Pain and suffering costs, if not compensated, provide strong incentives for individuals to avoid moral hazard problems. Still, full insurance always raises the possibility of an increased accident rate, and moral hazard is an important factor to consider when discussing any social policy issue that involves an insurance component.

One final point about moral hazard. Being insured may not only affect the behavior of the person insured, it may affect others. For example, one interesting study examines the prescription-writing tendencies of Swedish doctors with respect to brand-name versus generic drugs. When a brand-name drug has a generic counterpart, the two drugs generally provide identical therapeutic effects. The brand-name drug, however, typically is much more expensive. If there is no difference between the drugs other than their prices, doctors who continue to prescribe the brand-name drug are imposing higher costs either on their patients or on their patients' insurance providers.

The study finds that one indication (out of several) of a doctor's choice to prescribe the brand-name or generic drug depends on how much out-of-pocket cost for the drug is incurred by the patient, as opposed to incurred by the insurance provider. The greater the out-of-pocket cost to the patient, the less likely a doctor is to prescribe the brand-name drug. This suggests that doctors are less concerned with the overall cost of the treatment they provide when they know a third party insurer is bearing a large portion of the cost. This increases the insurance costs either to tax payers in a public health care system or to members of a private insurance pool. When the existence of insurance in and of itself provides incentives for costly, inefficient behavior, a moral hazard problem exists.

ECONOMISTS AND INFECTIOUS DISEASES

In April 2009, a serious outbreak of the H1N1 (swine) flu compelled governments around the world to respond immediately in various ways to help curtail the life-threatening virus. In Mexico City, all schools and universities were closed, and troops passed out filter masks outside the National Cathedral on Sunday morning. In addition, the Mexican government borrowed over $200 million from the World Bank, of which $180 million was earmarked for the highly open-ended use of building up strategic operational and institutional capacities to deal with the issue, while the rest of the loan was for medicine and medical equipment. The Russian government banned all pork imports from Mexico and the southern United States, and travelers from those areas landing in Russia were subject to having their temperature taken upon arrival. In Hong Kong, a team of scientists were called upon to try to find a quick test for the virus. Australia required airlines to identify any passengers exhibiting flu-like symptoms. And in the United States, the government declared a public health emergency, which allows federal, state, and local agencies to free up resources to help curtail the virus.

Perhaps the most controversial measure was the use of thermal-image scanners at airports to spot overheated travelers and have them checked for fever before they could infect others. Canada had invested in these heat scanners several years earlier to help curtail the SARS outbreak, but the machines were ultimately determined to be cost ineffective. But with the machines still sitting around airports, why not use them to fight the latest flu outbreak? With the machines paid for, however, there was still the issue of current costs imposed by the scanners. The scanners do not detect fever perfectly but allow for an indication of elevated skin temperature, and those who are flagged can then be pulled over and more thoroughly examined. The additional examination may include having your temperature checked, a closer look for other symptoms, an interview about your medical history, and questions about where you have recently traveled. In Indonesia, where they also used the machines, if you are flagged you may be sprayed with a 70 percent alcohol solution. And while these scanners do not detect individuals who are carrying the virus but do not yet exhibit symptoms, supporters of the scanners argue that it is a far more cost-effective method and less intrusive procedure than literally having doctors and nurses board planes to physically examine passengers.

While all these measures employ costly resources, it appears to be just plain common sense that society will reap tremendous benefits from halting the spread of highly infectious diseases. After all, if we divide the population into two groups—those who have contracted the disease and those who have not—it is a simple prediction that the probability of contracting the disease if you are in the second group is positively related to the size of the first group. This is known as a *positive hazard rate*, meaning that the more people who have the disease, the more likely it is for others to contract it. A positive hazard rate is fundamental to the field of *epidemiology*, defined as the study of populations in order to determine the frequency and distribution of disease, and to measure risks. And a positive hazard rate justifies rapid state involvement, as seen worldwide with the outbreak of swine flu.

But leave it to economists to mess up a good thing by sticking in the word *economic* where it typically doesn't belong, such as with the fairly new field of inquiry known as *economic epidemiology*. And the first economic challenge to common sense in this field is to reconsider the belief that the hazard rate is positive. Perhaps it is just the opposite, such that the larger the fraction of infected people in the population, the *less likely* it is for others to contract the disease. If the hazard rate is indeed negative, the justification for rapid state intervention to eradicate infectious diseases may become less compelling.

Why might the hazard rate be negative? It is possible that individuals who have not yet been infected will have the incentive to take *private* precautions to prevent future infection, and the incentive to take these precautions will be *stronger* the larger the fraction of infected people in the population. To combat the swine flu, individuals may decide to restrict their own travel plans, choose to wear a protective mask, get a flu shot, enhance their daily hygiene regimen, and numerous other precautions that anyone can undertake without the aid of state intervention. Recently, economists have examined how private precautions can be adopted to prevent the spread of AIDS. Two studies illustrate the concept well.

The first study looks at how the prevalence of AIDS affects condom use by looking at a state-by-state variation of condom use prior to the onset of the disease and then after the disease progressed. The study finds that there was little variation in condom use across states prior to the disease but much variation afterwards, and that variation was directly related to the prevalence of the disease. States in which the disease was more prevalent saw higher condom-use rates, especially among young single men (ages 25 to 27) living in urban areas, a group predicted to face a greater risk of contracting AIDS than other demographic groups.

The second study pushes the argument a little bit further into the "thinking outside the box" category. It might not be much of a stretch to argue that to reduce the probability of you contracting AIDS, you reduce the amount of sex you have in terms of either number of partners or frequency. You may even decide to abstain from sex completely. But, would you change your sexual preference specifically to avoid contracting AIDS? This study argues that you very well might.

Here's the story. First, if you are a man it is a fact that you are far more likely to contract AIDS from having sex with a man than with a woman. The study provides some numbers for that result, showing that it is *thousands* of times more likely that a man would get AIDS from having sex with a man than with a woman. Furthermore, it holds the same for women, as it is more likely a woman would get AIDS from having sex with a man than with a woman. Quite simply, having sex with a man is more risky than having sex with a woman, regardless of your gender. Put all this together and there is the theoretical possibility that to reduce the likelihood of contracting AIDS, as the prevalence of AIDS increases, some men may change their sexual preference from homosexual to heterosexual, and some women may change their sexual preference from heterosexual to homosexual. The study's empirical results support the theory.

Just because there are private precautions that can be taken to help reduce the impact of an infectious disease, that does not rule out the role of state intervention, it just requires us to think carefully about the intricate relationship between the two. Public expenditure and private expenditure to eradicate disease may be *substitutes* for each other. For example, if individuals purchase their own condoms to practice safe sex, there is less justification to involve public resources to achieve the same goal. While both private and public resources may have better uses elsewhere, private resources (at least as a first pass) tend to be used efficiently, because individuals have the direct incentive to use their resources to their own best use. Social resources, on the other hand, are used by policy officials not for their own best use, but for the best use of others, making it far more difficult to determine whether the resources are used efficiently. Nevertheless, private resources can be used inefficiently from a *social* perspective, and, for example, if high school students are not practicing safe sex because they choose not to purchase condoms, there may very well be a role for public policy to provide condoms to these students. The important point is that if private resources are being drawn into the fight against disease, there may be less need to further draw in public resources.

On the other hand, it is also possible that private and public expenditure may *complement* each other. Maybe high school students would purchase condoms if they truly understood how effective they can be in preventing the spread of disease. In this case, public resources used to administer an informational campaign in high schools, for example, can work in tandem with the private resources that will be encouraged to be devoted to safe sex practices. In all, it is highly unlikely that the efficient way to eradicate disease is only through private expenditure or only through public expenditure. But the question of what role social policy should play, or could play for that matter, in either encouraging or discouraging private investment in disease prevention remains open.

ECONOMISTS AND HIV/AIDS

As part of the research on infectious diseases, economists have begun to devote a lot of time to studying the HIV/AIDS epidemic. To be expected, economists have some unusual ideas, at least when compared to health research undertaken by scholars in several other disciplines. The goal here is to highlight just a sampling of these ideas.

A Little Knowledge Can Be a Dangerous Thing

One of the leading weapons in the fight against the spread of HIV is information. To encourage individuals to get blood tests, one form of social intervention is to have the government subsidize the cost of the tests. The commonsense argument is that if people are aware of their HIV status, they will be able to adjust their behavior appropriately and prevent the additional spread of the disease. One interesting study, however, argues that just the opposite may happen—information about HIV status may lead to an *increase* in the spread of the disease.

If you don't know your HIV status, a blood test will inform you whether you are HIV positive or negative. How will you respond to this information? The answer depends on what you think your HIV status is *before* you take the test. For example, let's assume you are a very low-risk individual and believe you are HIV negative. If the blood test confirms your belief, there is no reason to expect much change in your behavior: you're not really learning anything new. But let's say the blood test reveals that you are HIV positive. In this case, you are in a higher risk category than you thought you were. This new information may change your behavior and help you reduce the spread of the disease. This is precisely the thinking behind encouraging blood tests.

Now let's assume you are a very high-risk individual and believe you are HIV positive. If the blood test confirms your belief, once again there is no reason to expect much change in your behavior. But if the blood test reveals that you are HIV negative, you are actually in a lower risk category than you thought you were. In this case, the new information may change your behavior by prompting you to take more risks, and this may help spread the disease. The authors of the study present some empirical evidence to support this unusual claim.

Using survey data from individuals who were required to have a blood test to participate in the study, they were able to determine which individuals knew their HIV status before the test (the control group), and which individuals learned their HIV status because of the test. Sexual promiscuousness was measured by comparing the number of sexual partners one year prior to the test to the number of partners one year after the test. What they found was that individuals who learned what they already believed didn't significantly change their behavior. Individuals who learned they were HIV positive when they believed they were HIV negative did reduce their number of sexual partners. This group, however, was a very small proportion of the total sample. Individuals who learned they were HIV negative when they believed they were HIV positive did increase their number of sexual partners. Thus, the authors concluded that it was possible that the subsidized testing for HIV may actually increase the spread of the disease.

Although it is just a single study, and the empirical evidence is far from definitive, I believe the main point of the study has nothing to do with the empirical results. The commonsense belief that more HIV testing will help reduce the spread of the disease may not be accurate. At least the theoretical possibility exists that offsetting behavior may lead to results that are totally at odds with the intention of subsidized blood tests.

The tricky role of the behavioral response to new information in terms of social policy was also discussed in chapter 5 with respect to smoking. If smokers tend to overestimate the risks of smoking, they may be smoking less than they would if they were perfectly informed. With the HIV study, individuals who believe they are in a high-risk category may be less sexually promiscuous than they would be if they were perfectly informed. Is it sound social policy to provide accurate information if that can lead to an *increase* in risky behavior? That is a difficult question to answer, but understanding the role of behavioral responses to social policy can help lead to better-informed policy.

Miracle Drugs versus Human Behavior

In 1996 and 1997, some powerful new drugs to combat the impact of HIV were introduced. Although HIV drugs had been available for years, none were deemed overly effective. That all changed, especially with the introduction of a class of drugs known as protease inhibitors. The benefits of these drugs were felt immediately, and by the end of 1997 the quality of life for HIV-infected patients greatly improved. Mortality rates decreased, as did the adverse consequences of living with the disease. While expenditures on prescription drugs sharply increased, other inpatient and outpatient medical expenses sharply declined. However, as the drugs extended the life expectancy of those with HIV, they would be using health care resources (either public or private) for a longer amount of time. One economic study, putting all of the costs and benefits of these new drugs together, found that the benefits, in terms of reducing mortality rates, improving the quality of life, and reducing medical expenditures, substantially outweighed the costs of using the drugs. The drugs, if not a miracle cure for HIV, were certainly capable of efficiently reducing the severe costs of the disease. Or were they?

What one study hails as a phenomenal success story, another study, while not completely refuting that claim, does highlight some less optimistic outcomes of the HIV drugs. When new drugs are introduced that offer substantial benefits in combating a disease, the potential for offsetting behavior can be serious. The HIV drugs do not eradicate the disease. Instead, they reduce the mortality rate and improve the quality of life for those who have contracted the disease. How can that impact the behavior of those with HIV? First, the costs of contracting HIV have fallen, which may reduce the fear of contracting the disease in the first place. That may lead to more risky behavior. Second, if these drugs lower the average concentration of the virus, the risk of spreading or contracting the disease *per risky act* has fallen, and this may lead to more risky behavior. Third, as life expectancy increases for those who have contracted HIV, the longer life span may lead to a cumulatively greater number of risky acts. But keep in mind, if all this potential for offsetting behavior increases the prevalence of HIV, that in and of itself may lead people who do not have the disease to take more precautions to reduce the risk of contracting HIV. In all, the study concludes that if the new drugs have the unintended consequence of increasing the spread of the virus, it may be best to shift resources from research and development of these type of drugs toward effective vaccines instead, or toward prevention programs.

Abstinence versus AIDS Information Education

Among their many day-to-day stresses, teenagers have to deal with raging hormones. Promiscuous behavior among teens, however, may advance the spread of sexually transmitted diseases, HIV/AIDS included. Sexual education programs at school (and education at home) may help curtail the spread of diseases. If social resources are going to be devoted to provide students with information that will encourage them to make safer choices, exactly what would be the most effective type of information to disseminate?

Beginning in 2000, President George W. Bush's administration devoted millions of dollars for sexual education programs that embraced an abstinence-only approach. The logic is simple: if high school students can be taught to abstain from sex until later in life, the spreading of disease can be curtailed. Alternatively, students can be given AIDS information, especially with respect to how safe sexual practices, such as condom use, can help curtail the spread of disease. One criticism of this approach, however, is that if students are taught how to practice safer sex, fewer students may abstain from sex, because they now believe the risks are not as great. But safer sex does not imply 100 percent safe, thus more students having sex may lead to more disease spreading.

One study examines the effectiveness of the different education approaches and, while only a single study, finds some clear results. Most importantly, the abstinence-only campaign appeared to be counterproductive in terms of reducing the sexual behavior of students, but the AIDS education program did have an impact in getting sexually active students to use condoms more often. Furthermore, the AIDS education program did not seem to have an impact on the probability of abstaining from sex, suggesting that it was *not* encouraging more students to have sex. In all, the results of this study at least suggest that certain policy options, while strong in good intentions, may simply be ineffective and a waste of social resources.

Fighting HIV in Uganda: As Simple as ABC?

HIV prevalence in Africa is at an alarmingly high rate, and social policy designed to lower the disease rate has typically been, at best, disappointingly ineffective. But in the early 1990s, Uganda was unique among sub-Saharan African countries in that HIV prevalence declined sharply there. What was responsible for this success story? The Ugandan government began devoting resources to a comprehensive anti-HIV educational program, centered around a campaign known as ABC—Abstinence, Be faithful, and use Condoms. The program consisted of in-school education, billboard advertising, joint efforts with faith-based organizations, and so on. The program was deemed so successful that other African countries began to devote a substantial amount of resources to similar educational campaigns.

While these types of educational campaigns can affect individuals' sexual behavior and reduce the spread of HIV, there is always room for healthy skepticism in attributing dramatic changes in disease rates to education alone. And one study, interested in determining if other factors may have played a substantial role in Uganda's success story, argues that there may be another important reason why there was a sharp decline in HIV prevalence in the early 1990s—a concurrent decline in coffee prices!

There appears to be evidence that HIV in Africa spreads along trucking routes as goods are trucked from inland areas to coastal areas in preparation for export. The story goes like this. Male truckers, while away from home, tend to have many sexual encounters along their routes. These encounters are often with high risk sexual partners, such as prostitutes, who, as a group, are likely to have a high prevalence of HIV. As truckers continue along their routes, infection rates spread. Furthermore, when truckers return to their wives, they increase the spread of HIV at home, and this is further exacerbated if infected wives have extramarital affairs while their husbands are off on their routes. As trucking becomes more active when export rates are high, there is a potential link between the rate of exports and the prevalence of HIV.

In this study, a strong link is found between the value of exports and the spread of HIV, especially in Uganda in the period 1983 to 1997. Quantitatively, the study finds that a doubling of exports leads to a quadrupling of HIV infections. And in the early 1990s, the decline in the value of coffee exports (among other export declines) helps explain not all but a significant portion of the decline in the spread of HIV. No doubt, the educational campaign also played a role, but education is meant to change the personal *choices* of individuals, always a tricky proposition, whereas the decline of exports impacts their *opportunities*. But what does this suggest about a possible social policy intervention to curb the spread of HIV in Africa?

One can take the results of this study and suggest that an obvious policy stance is to reduce the rate of international trade with African countries. If fewer exports lead to lower prevalence of HIV, the disruption in the flow of trade may provide an unusual response in the fight against the disease. But on the other hand, if unrestricted trade can increase the wealth of African countries, it is well-established that wealthier countries have more resources to use to fight the spread of infectious diseases. Furthermore, the wealthier individuals are, the more resources they can privately use to protect themselves from disease. In all, this study provides an excellent example of the policy complexities involved in dealing with a difficult situation in an impoverished region of the world.

The HIV Criminal

Another approach to combating the spread of HIV is to impose criminal sanctions against those who knowingly spread the disease. In the United States, each state has criminal laws dealing with the spread of infectious diseases, so applying such laws to the spread of HIV is not new. However, many states have recently enhanced these laws specifically to deal with the HIV virus. The thinking involves standard economic reasoning: increase the cost of certain behaviors, and expect to see such behaviors reduced. As with all criminal acts, one important role of sanctions is to *deter* such behavior (as opposed to simply punishing an act already committed). By increasing the penalties associated with spreading HIV, by enforcing heavier sentences and/or by devoting more resources toward prosecuting such defendants, individuals with HIV are predicted to be less likely to engage in sexual acts without disclosing their health status. And with disclosure, either fewer sexual acts will occur or safer sex practices will be undertaken.

One study, indeed, finds that more aggressive prosecution does reduce the spread of HIV by directly making it more costly for those with the disease to engage in sexual acts without full disclosure. However, the study also argues there is an offsetting behavior that needs to be taken into account. To avoid the more severe sanctions of spreading HIV, it is possible that individuals will engage in riskier anonymous sexual acts. For example, if greater criminal sanctions drive some sexual behavior underground, such as increased encounters with prostitutes who, if infected by a client, are unlikely to be able to easily trace the disease back to a specific person, this riskier behavior may enhance the spread of HIV. This indirect effect of enhanced sanctions will work against the direct effect. Taken together, the study finds that the direct effect dominates the indirect effect, but the indirect effect does exist.

In all, economists have added some complex layers to the HIV/AIDS policy debate. Paying attention to how policy affects behavior is paramount in designing effective policies. This thinking will be further emphasized with the last topic for this chapter: the role of tort liability in effecting the behavior of firms in terms of product safety, and the behavior of doctors in terms of medical malpractice.

THE MARKET FOR SAFER PRODUCTS

Let me ask you a "how comfortable are you with the following idea" question: On a scale from 0 to 10, with 0 being the least comfortable and 10 being the most comfortable, how comfortable would you be living in a society in which firms faced absolutely no products liability law (or even government product safety regulations)—a world of complete caveat emptor? The most common answer I get from my students is 0. It just doesn't sound right to most people that firms would be adequately concerned with producing safe products if there were no laws that forced them to be concerned. If you were to ask professional economists the same question, however, I assure you that you would get some sincere answers of 10. Does that make you feel more comfortable?

One of the goals of product liability law is to provide incentives for firms to produce safe products. Without such law, it is often argued that consumers would be at the complete mercy of firms who place profit over safety. But even without product liability law, firms may find it in their best interest to provide safe products because of two concepts I discussed in earlier chapters—*full price* and *gains from trade*. When I discussed the risks associated with smoking, I argued that the full price of a pack of cigarettes is primarily made up of two components: the dollar amount that you have to pay, and a nonmonetary amount that reflects any potential risks you must bear. With no product liability laws, the consumer bears all product-related risks, so the full price the consumer pays typically exceeds the monetary price. To maximize gains from trade, then, the consumer is interested in paying the lowest full price for a product, *not* necessarily the lowest monetary price.

For example, assume you are considering buying an automatic garage door opener. There are two models to choose from that are identical except for one feature: the more expensive model includes a safety feature that prevents the door from lowering when anything is beneath it. The model without the safety feature costs you $1,000, and the model with the feature costs you $1,200. If the firm is not liable for any garage door–related accident, and you don't purchase the model with the safety feature, your *expected damages* are $300. In other words, if you face a 5 percent chance of suffering damages of $6,000, *on average* your damages are (5%)($6,000), or $300. With the safety feature, your expected damages are zero (that is, there is no longer a chance of the accident occurring). From your perspective, the full price of the garage door without the safety feature is $1,300, that is, $1,000 monetary price and $300 in expected damages. But with the safety feature, your full price is only $1,200. Thus, you pay a lower full price and receive an additional $100 in gains from trade if you purchase the model with the safety feature.

The main point is that if consumers have perfect information about the product risks they face, firms have the incentive to provide safety features when it is efficient to do so. Firms can compete against each other to provide safety features that consumers demand, and the firms that can maintain the lowest *full* prices will be most successful. But even when considering firms that enjoy some monopoly power, they too have an incentive to provide safety features when there are gains from trade to be exploited. Safety can be thought of as a product, just like any other product, and market forces can encourage its provision. But what if consumers misperceive the risks they face?

If consumers are not aware, or typically underestimate the product risks they face, firms may not have the correct incentive to provide safety features. With the garage door example, if you incorrectly believe there is no product risk without the safety feature, the less expensive model will also appear to have the lower full price. The monetary price of $1,000 is the full price, at least as far as you are concerned, so you would not want to purchase the $1,200 model with the safety feature. In this case, product liability law can provide the incentive for the firm to produce the model with the safety feature. Just how does product liability law impact the firm's behavior?

TO BE OR NOT TO BE STRICT

Product liability law is highly complex, and more than just a little confusing at times. Add in economic analysis, and then things get even more challenging. So I am simply going to introduce some basic ideas about two liability rules: *strict liability* and *negligence*. A rule of strict liability holds a firm liable for any product-related accident, regardless of how safe it was in producing its product. A rule of negligence, on the other hand, only holds a firm liable if it is determined it did not provide the "appropriate" safety features. More specifically, a firm must decide how much care to take in producing its product. Economists refer to the efficient amount of care as *due care*. A rule of strict liability holds a firm liable for damages without any consideration of how much care it took. A rule of negligence holds a firm liable for damages only if it took *less* than due care.

Let's return to the garage door example, but make one slight change. In the original example, if the firm adds the safety feature, it is assumed that no accident can occur. In general, however, safety features reduce the probability of an accident occurring but not all the way to zero. The safety feature may lower the probability of an accident occurring from 5 percent to 1 percent, and then it is either not technically possible to lower the probability to zero or far too expensive to do so. Whatever the case, we will now assume that it is efficient for the firm to add the safety feature that maintains the accident probability at 1 percent, and this is the due care level of safety. (Using the same numbers from above, for a cost of $200, the firm lowers the probability of the accident by 4 percent and therefore saves (4%) ($6,000), or $240, which makes the safety feature efficient to add.)

Under the strict liability rule, the firm has the incentive to provide the safety feature. If it doesn't, it will have to pay expected damages of (5%)($6,000), or $300. If it does, it incurs the additional safety cost of $200, and then will only be liable for (1%)($6,000), or $60, for a total additional cost (safety plus expected liability) of $260. In other words, for a cost of $200, the firm lowers its expected liability from \$300 to \$60, a saving of \$240, and that is worth doing. Thus, one advantage of holding the firm strictly liable for damages is that it provides it with the incentive to take due care. The firm, in effect, is forced to make a private decision that is perfectly matched to the correct social decision: the firm must trade-off the costs of additional safety with the benefits of additional safety. But notice, strict liability does not give the firm the incentive to reduce the accident rate to zero. That last 1 percent reduction will, by assumption, cost more than the (1%)(\$6,000), or \$60, it will save. The firm prefers to bear the expected liability of \$60 rather than incur the additional safety cost. (I am assuming that there are no legal costs the firm incurs. If there are legal costs, the firm may prefer to spend the additional amount on safety to save the \$60 expected liability *and* the additional legal costs.)

Under the negligence rule, the firm also has the incentive to provide the efficient safety feature but for a slightly different reason. In this case, the firm gets to *avoid* liability by taking due care, meaning that for the additional safety cost of \$200, the firm saves the full expected liability of \$300, which of course is worth doing. Under strict liability, the firm cannot avoid liability if an accident occurs, but it makes the correct decision to spend on safety when that reduces liability by a great enough amount. Both rules, then, provide the incentive for the firm to add the safety feature. So, in what ways do the rules differ?

One of the biggest differences between the two rules involves the amount of litigation each one is predicted to encourage. With strict liability, there can be a large number of claims against firms. Anyone who has suffered a product-related damage is likely to have a valid claim. Legal claims, and eventual trials if warranted, are very costly to pursue. And even if these costs are privately incurred by the opposing parties, it is legitimate to question whether there are other liability rules that can lead to cost-efficient safety efforts *without* the added burden of costly litigation. And negligence is one such rule. Under the negligence rule, a claim can only be successful against a firm that was taking less than due care. In theory, then, if the negligence rule provides the incentive for the firm to take due care, there should never be any successful claims against the firm. In practice, however, the negligence rule can be very difficult for the courts to apply.

To use strict liability, the court must determine that an accident occurred and that the accident was caused by the product. The court does not have to evaluate the level of safety effort the firm was undertaking. To use the negligence rule, the court must address two additional questions: What is the due care level of the firm, and how much *actual* care was the firm taking? These can be very difficult questions to answer. As I discussed in chapter 2 with the Ford Pinto case, product design entails hundreds if not thousands of decisions. How does the court determine optimal design? Even in the garage door example, to find due care the court has to determine the cost of adding the safety feature and the benefit in terms of reduced probability of an accident. Can the court correctly conclude that a 1 percent accident rate is optimal in this example? Observing the safety feature is not difficult—the garage door either has it or doesn't. But in many product liability settings, observing how much care a firm is taking, especially in setting up its manufacturing process, may be extremely difficult to do. In other words, there may be more claims under a strict liability rule, but the costs *per* claim of applying the rule are very low. This is an advantage of strict liability over negligence.

Because due care levels are likely to change over time with technological developments, another argument in favor of strict liability is that it provides the firm with the incentive to continually adopt new safety efforts. Because the firm can never avoid liability, it has the incentive to constantly reevaluate its production process to adopt new cost-efficient technology. With the negligence rule, the courts must constantly revise the meaning of due care, which will be a slow and difficult process. In this case, the firm may not have the incentive to improve its safety effort until it believes the courts will hold it negligent when using older technology.

The negligence rule does offer an advantage over strict liability in terms of affecting the *consumer's* behavior. Product-related accidents are not always only the fault of the manufacturer. For example, when using the automatic garage door, perhaps a consumer often runs under the door while it is closing. This may increase the probability of an accident occurring. Under the strict liability rule, the firm is liable for damages regardless of the behavior of the consumer. The consumer is fully compensated for damages, even though his behavior initiated the accident. This is the moral hazard problem in a slightly different setting than discussed earlier. If strict liability fully compensates the consumer, he has no incentive to take any additional care to reduce the probability of the accident. But under the negligence rule, if the firm takes due care, the consumer is either less likely to file a claim or less likely to prevail in court, thus putting the burden of damages upon himself. This is a big advantage of the negligence rule—it *simultaneously* provides the firm and the consumer the incentives to take due care. The firm takes due care to avoid liability, and the consumer takes due care to efficiently trade-off between safety costs and safety benefits.

Finally, there is one other problem with the negligence rule. As mentioned above, it can be a difficult and costly rule to apply, and it is quite possible for the courts to make mistakes in assessing due care levels and actual care levels. For example, what if the court mistakenly finds that a firm took due care when it did not? Or, what if the court mistakenly finds the firm did not take due care when it did? These types of mistakes are inevitable. What's more interesting, however, is precisely how firms will respond to the possibility that the courts misapply the negligence rule. To examine this issue, I will turn to the medical profession.

DOCTORS ON THE DEFENSE

Nobody likes to think about doctors behaving badly, but there has been a growing concern that the pressures of medical malpractice liability have led to a serious adverse behavioral response from doctors—they are providing *too much* care for their patients. Doctors being too careful, you say, impossible. Well, believe it or not, the US government doesn't find it impossible. The concept is known as *defensive medicine*, and it is well defined in a 1994 Office of Technology Assessment (US Congress) study:

> Defensive medicine occurs when doctors order tests, procedures, or visits, or avoid high-risk patients or procedures, primarily (but not necessarily solely) to reduce their exposure to malpractice liability. When physicians do extra tests or procedures primarily to reduce malpractice liability, they are practicing positive defensive medicine. When they avoid certain patients or procedures, they are practicing negative defensive medicine.

It doesn't seem like doctors could ever take too much care with their patients, but that is exactly what positive defensive medicine is concerned with. If the costs of extra medical resources outweigh the health benefits those resources lead to, too much care is being provided. With negative defensive medicine, too little care is being provided. In other words, procedures with benefits that outweigh their costs are not being provided. The key question, then, from an economic perspective is this: What is the *optimal* amount of medical care (in any given situation)? A real-world legal case provides an example of how this question may be answered.

In 1959, a 23-year-old woman visited her ophthalmologist, was diagnosed with nearsightedness, and was fitted with contact lenses. Through 1968, she routinely complained of eye irritation. Finally, in 1968, at the age of 32, she was given an eye pressure test that indicated she had glaucoma. By that time, she had suffered severe and permanent eye damage. The court had to address the question of whether the doctor's initial lack of early detection of glaucoma could be deemed malpractice.

At the time, it was standard practice in ophthalmology not to apply the pressure test for anyone under the age of 40. Although two lower courts ruled in favor of the doctor, the Supreme Court of

Washington state reversed the lower courts' decisions. Simply put, the supreme court believed that the benefit of applying the pressure test outweighed the small cost of the test:

> Under the facts of this case reasonable prudence required the timely giving of the pressure test to this plaintiff. The precaution of giving this test to detect the incidence of glaucoma to patients under 40 years of age is so imperative that irrespective of its disregard by the standards of the ophthalmology profession, it is the duty of the courts to say what is required to protect patients under 40 from the damaging results of glaucoma.

Although the court believed it was optimal to apply the pressure test as part of a routine eye exam regardless of the age of the patient, it may not have been optimal from a medical standpoint. At the time of the court's decision, an expert in the field of ophthalmology reached the opposite conclusion. He argued that the incidence of glaucoma was too low, and it would be an inefficient use of resources to make population screening the norm. If it is the case that it is not optimal to routinely apply the pressure test, the court's ruling could lead to the practice of defensive medicine. It may be far better for doctors to apply the test rather than face the possibility of substantial malpractice liability.

The practice of defensive medicine suggests that doctors may be inefficiently responding to the pressure of malpractice liability. Empirically, this can be a very difficult concept to verify or refute. Doctors may have many valid reasons for providing what may seem to be excessive care or inadequate care, and not solely as a response to malpractice liability. Two related studies by the same researchers shed some light on these issues.

In the first study, the authors look at cesarean-section delivery rates and infant health. A cesarean section is a fairly costly surgical procedure (relative to nonsurgical deliveries) that is generally best used when complications arise. If doctors are concerned about excessive malpractice liability in delivering babies that suffer adverse health outcomes, they may practice positive defensive medicine in using a delivery method that is more costly but provides less of a risk of a bad health outcome to the baby. And although it seems that it may always be a good idea to minimize the risk to the baby, as with any other bad outcome I have discussed in this book, there are trade-offs to consider. A cesarean section, as with any surgery, definitely has costs that may not be offset by its benefits, especially for what would be a normal delivery otherwise.

The authors investigate whether increased malpractice liability risk is associated with more cesarean sections but not better infant health outcomes. That would imply the costs of the increased cesarean sections have no offsetting health benefits, which suggests evidence of positive defensive medicine. If the increased rate of cesarean sections leads to better infant health outcomes, this makes the finding of positive defensive medicine less likely. One of the authors' conclusions is that they do find evidence of positive defensive medicine.

In the second study, the authors focus on the issue of negative defensive medicine in prenatal infant health care. They argue that fear of malpractice liability may delay prenatal care, thus implying the practice of negative defensive medicine. And if this delay leads to poorer infant health outcomes, it may be efficient to begin prenatal care at an earlier stage. In this case, the authors do find that while increased malpractice liability pressure does slightly delay prenatal care, it doesn't seem to have any effect on infant health outcomes. This suggests that there may be no evidence of negative defensive medicine in this particular setting.

Another interesting study examines the impact of medical malpractice liability on the frequency of cesarean sections by using a different approach than the above study. Instead of looking at infant health outcomes, the study examines how doctors respond to seeing either themselves or their colleagues confronted with a malpractice claim. The study finds that the threat of a lawsuit does increase the cesarean-section rate but only for a short period of time. This may be due to an initial overreaction to the lawsuit. In reality, doctors rarely lose these malpractice cases, and so they may soon discover that the threat of a lawsuit is not as costly as it first appears to be.

While the evidence is mixed as to the extent of defensive medicine, it is important to point out that when it comes to medical malpractice, product liability, or any other safety-related issue, when there is an *optimal* amount of care, too little care *or* too much care is not efficient. The old saying "It is better to err on the side of safety" may be memorable, but it is flawed. A better saying from an economic perspective may be "It is best not to err at all, but if you must make mistakes, make mistakes that lead to the smallest negative impact on social welfare." Admittedly, that is not very catchy, but it is sound economic reasoning.

NOTES

The seminal work on seat belt laws and offsetting behavior is by Sam Peltzman, "The Effects of Automobile Safety Regulation," *Journal of Political Economy* 83 (1975): 677–725. A more comprehensive discussion can be found in a book by Glenn Blomquist, *The Regulation of Motor Vehicle and Traffic Safety* (Boston, MA: Kluwer Academic Publishers, 1988).

W. Kip Viscusi provides several sources on the topic of behavioral responses to safety regulation. Two good books to start with are *Fatal Tradeoffs: Public and Private Responsibilities for Risk* (New York, NY: Oxford University Press, 1992), and *Rational Risk Policy* (Oxford: Oxford University Press, 1998).

Three articles on various aspects of moral hazard are by Jonathan Klick and Thomas Stratmann, "Subsidizing Addiction: Do State Health Insurance Mandates Increase Alcohol Consumption?" *Journal of Legal Studies* 35 (2006): 175–98; Dhaval Dave and Robert Kaestner, "Health Insurance and Ex Ante Moral Hazard: Evidence from Medicare," *International Journal of Health Care Finance and Economics* 9 (2009): 367–90; and Douglas Lundin, "Moral Hazard in Physician Prescription Behavior," *Journal of Health Economics* 19 (2000): 639–62.

I discuss several research papers on the topic of HIV/AIDS: On AIDS and condom use, see Avner Ahituv, V. Joseph Hotz, and Tomas Philipson, "The Responsiveness of the Demand for Condoms to the Local Prevalence of AIDS," *Journal of Human Resources* 31 (1996): 869–897. On AIDS and sexual preference, see Andrew M. Francis, "The Economics of Sexuality: The Effect of HIV/AIDS on Homosexual Behavior in the United States," *Journal of Health Economics* 27 (2008): 675–89. On HIV testing, see Michael A. Boozer and Tomas J. Philipson, "The Impact of Public Testing for Human Immunodeficiency Virus," *Journal of Human Resources* 35 (2000): 419–46. On HIV drugs, see Mark G. Duggan and William N. Evans, "Estimating the Impact of Medical Innovation: A Case Study of HIV Antiretroviral Treatments," *Forum for Health Economics and Policy* 11 (2008): 1–37; and Stephane Mechoulan, "Risky Sexual Behavior, Testing, and HIV Treatments," *Forum for Health Economics and Policy* 10 (2007) 1–49. On AIDS education, see Carol Horton Tremblay and Davina C. Ling, "AIDS Education, Condom Demand, and the Sexual Activity of American Youth," *Health Economics* 14 (2005): 851–67. On AIDS in Uganda, see Emily Oster, "Routes of Infection: Exports and HIV Incidence in Sub-Saharan Africa," *Journal of the European Economic Association* (forthcoming). On HIV and criminal sanctions, see Adeline Delavande, Dana Goldman, and Neeraj Sood, "Criminal Prosecution and HIV-Related Risky Behavior," *Journal of Law and Economics* 53 (2010): 741–82.

Two excellent sources on the economics of tort law that have influenced me greatly are by William M. Landes and Richard A. Posner, *The Economic Structure of Tort Law* (Cambridge, MA: Harvard University Press, 1987); and Steven Shavell, *Economic Analysis of Accident Law* (Cambridge, MA: Harvard University Press, 1987). Another interesting source specifically on products liability law is by W. Kip Viscusi, *Reforming Products Liability Law* (Cambridge, MA: Harvard University Press, 1991).

The US Congress, Office of Technology Assessment study is titled "Defensive Medicine and Medical Malpractice," OTA-H-602, July 1994.

The citation for the ophthalmologist malpractice case is Helling v. Carey, 83 Wash. 2d 514 (1974). For more on medical malpractice, see the text by Werner Z. Hirsch, *Law and Economics: An Introductory Analysis*, 2nd ed. (Boston, MA: Academic Press, 1988), chap. 7.

The studies on defensive medicine and infant health care are both by Lisa Dubay, Robert Kaestner, and Timothy Waidmann, "The Impact of Malpractice Fears on Cesarean Section Rates," *Journal of Health Economics* 18 (1999): 491–522; and "Medical Malpractice Liability and Its Effect on Prenatal Care Utilization and Infant Health," *Journal of Health Economics* 20 (2001): 591–611.

The study on the impact of malpractice liability on obstetricians is by David Dranove and Yasutora Watanabe, "Influence and Deterrence: How Obstetricians Respond to Litigation against Themselves and Their Colleagues," *American Economic Review* 12 (2010): 69–94.

One other interesting empirical study on medical malpractice is by Frank A. Sloan and John H. Shadle, "Is There Empirical Evidence for 'Defensive Medicine'? A Reassessment," *Journal of Health Economics* 28 (2009): 481–91.

The fine collection of survey articles in Anthony J. Culyer and Joseph P. Newhouse, eds., *Handbook of Health Economics* (Amsterdam: Elsevier, 2000) covers most of the topics in this chapter, as well as many other topics.

8   *There Are No Solutions*

WHERE WERE YOU when the lights went out on the East Coast and throughout parts of the Midwest on August 14, 2003? I was fortunate not to lose power, so I was able to watch some of the news coverage of the situation. Most of the early news focused on the human interest aspects of the blackout—people stuck in subways, tourists sleeping on the sidewalks, thousands of pedestrians walking home—and on trying to identify what caused the problem. Before too long, however, the experts were called in to discuss the solution to the problem, even before anyone precisely knew what the problem was.

There were basically two broad categories of solutions. The first was that the blackout was due to government regulation of the electric power industry. The industry needed to be deregulated so that the power companies could earn sufficient profit, allowing them to invest in better technology. The second category also agreed that government regulation was the problem, but the solution was to impose *more* regulatory control over the industry. All the experts did agree, however, that there would be huge rate increases in our electric bills.

I am no expert on the electric power industry, and I have only a rudimentary understanding of why my light comes on when I flick a switch, so I am making no claim that I have an educated opinion on how to deal with the blackout problem. But had I been asked for my professional opinion during the early hours of the blackout, I would have had a completely different take on the situation. I would have raised only one question: What is the optimal blackout rate?

Almost every expert pointed out that after the last major blackout in 1977 the public was assured that, after the subsequent improvements were made in the system, there would *never* be another major blackout. Well, that turned out not to be the case. Without missing a beat, almost every expert now argued that ultimately billions of dollars would have to be spent to update the system so that *this time* the problem would never happen again. Now as impressive as that claim is, I simply don't believe it. I doubt it is technically feasible to reduce the blackout rate completely to zero. And even if it is technically feasible, I have another question: *Is it worth it?*

There is no doubt that a massive blackout imposes substantial costs on society. Yet if billions are spent only to slightly reduce the blackout rate, the costs of reducing the rate may far exceed the *expected* benefits of reducing the rate. For example, let's assume a blackout imposes substantial social costs of $500 billion, and that an investment of only $25 billion can be spent to completely eliminate the blackout rate. This appears to be an excellent investment. But if the original blackout rate is 1 percent, and the new blackout rate is zero, that $25 billion investment doesn't save $500 billion but instead, *on average*, saves only 1 percent of $500 billion, or $5 billion. There simply may be no cost-effective way to completely eliminate the occasional blackout. And although it sounds very strange to argue that there is a positive optimal rate of power blackouts, it may very well be the case.

I believe the blackout issue provides an example of how a tragedy, in and of itself, may dictate public policy responses. As I discussed in chapter 2, it is important to detach yourself from the horror of a tragedy before considering appropriate policy solutions. I found it interesting that I didn't hear a single analyst conclude that maybe the best response would be to have no response at all. Just one major blackout in 26 years is pretty impressive. We may very well be able to get things back to normal and go another 26 years before another problem occurs. On the other hand, maybe there is a problem that needs to be fixed now, even at a substantial cost. What is the correct solution? Is there a *correct* solution?

THERE ARE ONLY TRADE-OFFS

I once heard an economist offer the following universal policy advice: *there are no solutions; there are only trade-offs*. My interpretation of that comment is that no matter what policy solution is offered for any particular social issue, that solution will never be satisfactory to everyone. There will always be trade-offs—costs and benefits—that make the concept of a "solution" ambiguous at best. Even with an accurate measurement of the costs and benefits, you still have to deal with the problem of defining social welfare and identifying a policy objective.

I have a friend whose job puts him in a position to provide policy advice that could possibly have real-world impact. I once asked him how comfortable he was being in that position, and he had no qualms at all about it. He then asked me the following question: If policy decisions have to be made, wouldn't you be happier having them made by economists than by anyone else? That's a good question, and after thinking about it for a few minutes, I decided that no, I wouldn't be happier. If economists were making all the policy decisions, we would never be given credit when things turned out well, but we would quickly be blamed when things turned out badly. Who needs that kind of pressure? Not me, but I know plenty of economists who would enjoy nothing more than having their advice taken seriously. But exactly how good is economic policy advice?

Let's take a highly controversial issue like the death penalty, and assume that policy officials are looking toward economists to provide sound policy advice. The death penalty is a complex issue, and there are several costs and benefits of its application that may be considered. There is also a vast range of emotional issues that can make the policy objective very difficult to identify. Some people would consider it repugnant for the state to ever take a life, period. No identification of benefits can ever matter to them. But let's keep it simple. Most economists would identify, in theory, one main benefit of applying the death penalty—it can deter murder.

The economic approach to crime typically starts with a rational criminal, whose actions can be swayed by changing the costs and benefits of committing crimes, even murder. If the death penalty is considered by the criminal to be a harsher penalty than the next alternative, usually a lifetime prison sentence, the more severe punishment imposes higher costs on criminal behavior thus, in theory, reducing such behavior. This is known as the *deterrent effect*—with each convicted murderer executed, fewer murders will occur. Thus, it is not just punishing a past criminal act that matters but also trying to discourage future criminal acts. It is not the only benefit of using the death penalty, and it still must be weighed against whatever costs there are, but I truly believe the vast majority of economists would accept the deterrent effect as the single most important benefit to consider when providing policy advice. So ask an economist about whether the deterrent effect actually exists. The answer depends upon which economist you ask.

For example, here is a small sampling of two opinions from economists who have spent a serious amount of time and energy studying the deterrent effect of the death penalty:

> Recent empirical studies have shown, without exception, that capital punishment deters crime. Using large data sets that combine information from all fifty states over many years, the studies show that, on average, an additional execution deters many murders. (Joanna Shepherd, *Michigan Law Review*, 2005)
>
> The US data simply do not speak clearly about whether the death penalty has a deterrent or anti-deterrent effect. The only clear conclusion is that execution policy drives little of the year-to-year variation in homicide rates. As to whether executions raise or lower the homicide rate, we remain profoundly uncertain. (John J. Donohue III and Justin Wolfers, *Stanford Law Review*, 2005)

Some death penalty studies have found the deterrent effect to exist, while others have found no such effect. These empirical studies that reach opposing conclusions are not just used for academic purposes—they enter into the public debate over the death penalty. But how useful are they if there isn't anything even close to a consensus concerning the deterrent effect? Any policy position can be supported with *some* peer-reviewed published study.

If you think I am painting economics in a bad light, I am not. These empirical studies have little to do with the way economists use economic reasoning to address the pros and cons of the death penalty. Economists generally agree on the fundamental *theoretical* trade-offs associated with the death penalty. Also, they often agree on the definition of social welfare, as well as on the objective of social welfare maximization. But even with these agreements, they can disagree on the measurement, either formally or informally, of the appropriate costs and benefits.

In chapter 1, I discussed the difficulties of doing empirical research to measure trade-offs. To the extent that these difficulties lead to differences in the way economists measure costs and benefits, these differences do not depict a shortcoming in economic reasoning. Personally, I believe that when it comes to many of the social issues discussed in this book, there are not many fundamental differences among most economists in the way they think about them. The differences that do exist often can be traced to the way economic reasoning typically must be quantified to make it applicable to real-world issues.

Because of the difficulties involved in finding definitive policy solutions, many economists choose to adopt a consistent policy viewpoint across many issues. For example, some economists believe that markets almost always work, while others believe that markets rarely work. Some economists believe that if markets fail, they fail for reasons that cannot be alleviated by government intervention. Others believe that market failures *require* government intervention. Other economists, myself included, tend to take an issue by issue approach to public policy. I believe that markets have advantages and disadvantages relative to government intervention policies, and these trade-offs are often issue-specific. The bottom line is that opposing policy positions are unavoidable due to the open-ended nature of policy analysis. This holds true not only for economists but for public policy scholars in any discipline.

IN MY OPINION, MY OPINION DOESN'T MATTER

When I teach policy courses, I often get asked by my students to discuss my personal opinions about the social issues we study. There's never any reason for me to do that, because my personal opinions have absolutely no bearing on what I want my students to learn in my courses. Furthermore, I'm not even sure I still have many personal opinions that can be distinguished from my professional opinions. I've been thinking about trade-offs for so many years that I rarely choose sides in an issue. I try to follow the mantra I teach my students, and I have mentioned earlier in this book—*if you are on one side of an issue, you are on the wrong side.* I've always liked the way that sounds.

Instead of presenting my personal opinions about the social issues I've discussed in this book, I will summarize my approach to thinking about such issues. When considering personal risk-taking activities that do not adversely affect others, such as the individual decision to smoke, drink, or overeat, I think it is very challenging to justify social intervention to control such behavior. Behavioral economists have made some great advances in cataloging situations in which paternalistic policies can truly be welfare improving, but these often rely on the open-ended concept of ideal preferences, meaning that social welfare is defined outside of the true preferences of the individuals being protected. Protecting people from themselves with interventionist policies is about as tricky as public policy can get. I can't say I'm comfortable with paternalistic policies, but I can certainly say I welcome the challenge of considering all the intricate costs and benefits such policies have to offer.

Where economics has an older and more fully developed approach to public policy is in dealing with situations in which individuals take actions that bother others. Private decisions can impose social costs on others, and this is exactly what laws are designed to deal with. In dealing with these issues, I do have a bias. I believe that the place to start is with the possibility of a market solution. Can the issue of smoking in bars and restaurants be handled by market forces? Can product safety decisions be motivated by market forces? If yes, the costs of choosing and implementing social control policies may be avoided. Furthermore, market forces may have the ability to achieve the efficient outcome without anyone having to know exactly what that outcome is. This is a tremendous advantage of a free market.

A market solution, however, is neither necessary nor sufficient to achieve a socially efficient outcome. It is not necessary because there can be other ways to allocate resources, such as with kidney exchanges to facilitate organ transplants or with fair use to circumvent copyright protection. It is not sufficient because there may be market failures, such as transactions costs or imperfect information, that prevent the efficient allocation of resources from being achieved. A free market is a means to an end, not an end in and of itself.

It is obvious that using economic reasoning is not the only way to approach social issues, but I have met many economists who argue that it is the best way to think about them. Although I personally use economic reasoning when I think about social issues, I find it difficult to apply the word *best* to ways of thinking about the world. How one thinks about social issues is a subjective concept. I do believe, however, that economic reasoning is an important and valid way to think about public policy, and I hope that I have been able to convey that to you throughout this book. I try to teach my students to be comfortable with economic reasoning, but I do not teach them to accept it outside the scope of my courses. That is something they have to make a personal decision to do. My hope is that even if they don't accept economic reasoning, they at least understand enough of it to appreciate why they don't accept it.

Actually, I tend to worry more about the students who embrace economic reasoning too quickly. When I taught at Texas A&M University in College Station, Texas, a fairly conservative town, I once gave a lecture about the trade-offs associated with legalizing prostitution and drugs. There was a student in my class who, at the time, was a student teacher at a local middle school. He so enjoyed my lecture about the economics of sex and drugs that he decided to present it to his class of adolescents. That was his last day of student teaching at that school! I guess I forgot to mention to him that, as a teacher of controversial issues, it is important to know your audience.

DARE TO DREAM

Obviously, policy decisions must be made. What it is that policy officials actually care about is a wide-open question. At one extreme, you can argue that policy officials are selfish and care only about their own best interests. I know many economists who are very comfortable with this position. At the other extreme, you can argue that policy officials care only about the well-being of others. I don't know *any* economists who are comfortable with this position. My guess is that policy officials care about politics, and so they probably care a little bit about everything that you can imagine.

If I got to pick my version of a perfect policy world, I would like policy officials to explicitly recognize the concept of trade-offs. For example, concerning an issue such as banning smoking in bars and restaurants, I would applaud a politician for making the following statement:

> I have decided to support the ban on smoking in all public bars and restaurants. I feel that this will greatly benefit nonsmokers from being bombarded with the deadly cigarette smoke of others. I recognize that smokers may be hurt by this policy by having their freedom to smoke curtailed. I also recognize that bar and restaurant owners may lose out if this policy reduces the profitability of their businesses. However, recognizing that there will be winners and losers to this policy, I sincerely believe that the benefits of this policy outweigh the costs.

Unfortunately, you would be much more likely to hear the following:

> I have decided to support the ban on smoking in all public bars and restaurants. I feel that this will greatly benefit nonsmokers from being bombarded with the deadly cigarette smoke of others. I also feel that this will benefit smokers who will now have fewer social opportunities in which to smoke, and this can only improve their health. This policy will also benefit bar and restaurant owners, because their businesses will soar in profitability due to the large potential customer base of nonsmokers who will now, without hesitation, gladly patronize smoke-free establishments. I apologize if I have failed to recognize any other group of individuals who are also going to benefit from this policy.

I guess I can take solace in the fact that if the former statement was the more realistic of the two, it wouldn't have been as much fun to write this book.

NOTES

The quote "there are no solutions, there are only trade-offs" was made by Thomas Sowell at a talk he gave at Ohio University in 1992.

For a fuller discussion of the economic approach to the death penalty, as well as other crime issues, see my book *The Economics of Crime: An Introduction to Rational Crime Analysis* (Oxon, UK: Routledge, 2008).

Index